FROM HEROIN TO HERESY

FROM HEROIN TO HERESY

THE MAKING OF AN AMERICAN SOCIAL THINKER

James E. Palombo

with

Phil Pisani

WN
WILLIAM
· NEIL ·
Publishing

Binghamton, New York

Published by William Neil Publishing, 4 Linclon Avenue, Binghamton, New York, 13905-4320.

Printed in the United States of America.

Library of Congress Control Number: 00-133010

ISBN: 0-9642806-4-7

Dedicated to our parents:

Ann and Mario Palombo
and
Marie and Ralph Pisani

CONTENTS

ACKNOWLEDGMENTS

As two neighborhood pals who have shared a number of experiences, reaching the point of completing a book and thanking those who have helped along the way truly represents something special. In thinking of the number of faces, especially in light of the accompanying emotions that their images present, there is no doubt that both of us sense how lucky we have been.

To the Kushner kids, Ann and her sister Auntie "I", Joanie and Ray Golden, and especially Kathy, Michael and Alyssa Pisani, all of whom had to continually listen to our discussions on what we would and wouldn't say in the next chapter.

To those in and around education: Terry Hubert, Randy Sheldon, Richard Quinney, Gene Sahs, Tom Johnson, Dave Duffee, Kevin Wright, and our sixth grade teacher Mrs. Marko, all of whom offered their time and effort in making this book work.

To Kathleen Mrva, our informal editor, who helped in making this book readable, Elisabeth Moser in Austria, and Maria Sestito-Stefanoni, Joe DeAngelo and Alcide Cicuto in Italy. Their graciousness contributed to the writing process.

To William Neil Publishers, who had the confidence and insight to support a book of this nature and Katie Ellis, our editor, who knew just what to do.

And, to the greater powers that be, for giving us the energy and the spirit and the health to develop what was once only an idea.

We salute you, and hope that the next round will be as rewarding as this one.

Jim & Phil

FORWARD

    I have known Jim Palombo for about twenty years now. We met while he was in prison and I, fortunately, had something to do with the change in his life pattern. This happened as we developed a post-secondary education program while he was incarcerated. Jim and I have stayed in touch through the years, mostly from afar, as he journeyed from one part of the world to another. When I learned that he was writing an "autobiographical discourse," I was very anxious to read it. After looking through the first draft, I was convinced that his story, especially as it was linked with his varied experiences with America's social problems, was one worth telling.

    Using a clear and engaging style, Jim brings to light a perspective that is at once insightful and easy to follow. In a challenging and informative way, he provides an opportunity for all of us to stop and reflect upon the kind of society we currently have, and the kind of society we wish to be. Palombo's book is in fact unique among today's contemporary works. Certainly there have been a good number of authors who have related prison experiences to the world at large, and particularly of the injustices that exist. I have only to cite the powerful writings of individuals like George Jackson, Eldridge Cleaver, and Malcolm X. But, this is not a story of a life-long criminal, nor about someone bent on revolutionary change. Rather, it is a story about a life-long American—someone born and raised in the changing times of America's last half century whose involvement with crime is only a part of the story and whose imprisonment actually sets off a journey to better understand America.

There is a significant correlation between what Jim relays in this book to what Tocqueville told us some one hundred and seventy years ago. I say this not to offer a comparison of the writers, but more to underscore the point that the offerings of both writers tell us a great deal about the "American experiment." Both relate to an individual's observations as he travels in and around America's attempt at democracy, although Palombo certainly has the advantage of almost two centuries, as well as that of being a genuine American.

However, there is another difference between the two, another advantage for Palombo if you will. Jim's inquiries begin with an attachment to the writings of Karl Marx, something that was not possible for Tocqueville. Sparked by a book given to him by his prison counselor (*The Critique of Legal Order*, by one of the foremost criminologists of our time, Richard Quinney), Palombo begins to examine America through the lens of a radical thinker. While in prison, and via the scholarship of many famous writers (Locke, Rousseau, Hobbes, etc., as well as Marx, Lenin, Trotsky, etc.), Jim follows the logic of Marx into a critical appraisal of American capitalist society. He begins to analyze the problems of our modern justice system within the context of political and economic variables, and, although not without internal and personal dilemma, he comes to see America as a place consumed by the elements of capitalism.

Given his new-found perspective, Palombo sets out from prison to "make the system" better. Importantly, there is a transformation of sorts here, in that his radical position becomes more focused on simply getting that position understood, rather than on trying to impose its tenets on the system. For Jim, then, the understanding of the position and the creation of a dialogue that involves that understanding will serve the ends of making America a better place.

With this desire in mind, his struggles throughout the book provide real-life drama, drama that all of us should be able to relate to, and that all of us should be concerned with. In fact, many of the problematic concerns that Jim raises point to the academic world that I occupy. In this world, one that has been provided the gift of free and open discussion of ideas and one filled with access to information perhaps unprecedented in the civilized world, Jim finds some disturbing contradictions. These contradictions exist between the goals of scientific research (this book itself actually represents an alternative to our more commonly accepted "Ivory Tower" research) and the goals of teaching and community service. Simply put, the goals of the latter often, and continually more so, take a backseat to the former. But, more importantly, the contradictions exist between what we preach about America and what we practice.

For Jim, it becomes incumbent that, in terms of substantive information, we begin to integrate into our educational process more of the ideas relevant to a critical analysis of capitalism. This he contends will not only help us to understand America more clearly, but, as importantly, will bring the significance of civic responsibility back to a position of prominence—something Jim cites as problematically lacking in today's educational endeavors.

After documenting his experiences in both Europe and Asia, experiences that provide him with, among other things, a better sense of being an American, Jim expresses his distress and frustration over what is occurring in our country. He writes in his conclusion that "we are indeed in some form of national identity crisis...where we seem afraid to recognize the identity we see before us, denying we are part of it, denying our ability to make any difference, denying any need to confront what we see." And, he references what he calls most "illogical" circumstances "where the political arena clearly doesn't represent the people's interests (money is such a factor in moving politicians and legislation that you're a fool to think otherwise), and where less than 50 percent of the people vote for our leaders and even fewer trust our government." For Jim, these troublesome observations are all too common to the American public.

At the end of the book, and mirroring his own belief that nothing positive can occur in America without an informed and educated public, he closes with the words of Thomas Jefferson: that "we must enlighten the people...educate and inform the whole mass of people...enable them to see that it is in their interest to preserve peace and order...they are the only sure reliance for the preservation of our liberty." These are powerful words that support the theme that Jim advances throughout the book; that being informed means understanding as much as we can about our collective selves...including what a capitalist system can and cannot support.

In my view, *From Heroin to Heresy, The Making of An American Social Thinker* makes an important and timely contribution to understanding the world in which we live. It is a story of one man who works to integrate his politicization via Marxist views with the realities of trying to make positive changes in our society. From his crime and prison days, to the development of his "formal" education, to helping immigrants, drug users and prisoners, to his experiences in foreign countries, Palombo presents a thought-provoking tale, and I am sure you will enjoy the reading. You are about to become involved with a particular kind of journey, and I feel confident in saying that once you begin this journey, you will be interested until its end. And, hopefully, as Jim would most assuredly want, you will be affected beyond that point.

Randall G. Shelden, Chair
Criminal Justice Department
University of Nevada, Las Vegas

PREFACE

      To begin, let me explain why this book is being written. As is the case with ideas, a certain need must be present for them to reach a point of actualization. For me the need is now and my point of actualization is this book, which I hope you will read, debate and enjoy.

      The need to write this book developed in a two-fold sense. First, I currently have a desire to put forth my thoughts and ideas on certain issues and concerns that I have been struggling with for some time. For years, students, colleagues and acquaintances have encouraged me to more publicly discuss these problems, issues and concerns in a way I generally reserve for the classroom. And, now, I feel I've traveled enough, seen enough, talked enough and thought enough—so it's time to write.

      Secondly, and on point with it being the right "time," what I hear today via personal conversation, classroom discussion or from the media is a sense of confusion and frustration about what is happening in America...What is going on with our political structure, our legal system, education, the family? How are we going to address these concerns as well as those of crime, poverty, homelessness, substance abuse, unemployment and staying competitive in the world market? Do we have the political and economic strategies to develop policies to address all these issues? Is the American public aware of what they are? Does it possess the "analytical tools" to understand what they are or what alternatives might be possible? Does the American public really care anymore? In an ironic sense then, the confusion and frustration of the day have also provided me with encouragement. They have fueled the inspiration for me to finally write about my thoughts on these matters, hoping this will help in sorting out the problems we face.

The concerns implicit in the above questions are, no doubt, heavy-handed. And, I am not proposing that absolute responses to them lie completely within this book. What I do suggest, however, is that much of what is contained here can contribute to a better understanding of what might be happening in America and why. Readers will certainly debate what is discussed in this book and may refute the points made. But, this is good because this book represents an attempt to develop and fuel a public dialogue, a dialogue that, through my years of trouble and struggle, I have come to perceive as crucial to America's future.

Therein lies the "why" of this book's offering. But there is more explaining to do so that the substance of this book, the "what" of the book, is clear. At the outset, I should note that what I have come to know and believe in developed via a late-blossoming educational process that converged with my experiences in life. This meant that I was capable of visualizing my life experiences in the context of many academic variables, a sort of "practical intellectualization" process that might never have occurred had this convergence not taken place.

Let me briefly review this convergence process, as it is most important in understanding what this book is about. I am an ex-convict, sentenced in 1977 to the Nevada State Prison System for the sale of heroin. And, although this book speaks to a variety of circumstances that come with prison life, this, in and of itself, is not of primary import. Why? Because during my prison stay something of greater significance happened. While in prison I was able to develop an educational program that allowed me to complete my bachelor's degree in political science. This educational program allowed me to formulate an analysis about what was going on in America, something I had no doubt thought about before, but only on a "street" level. The process, with its emphasis on comparative political and economic ideologies, helped to commingle my street thoughts on America with ideas organized by more academic "thinkers."

This process, filled with historical and philosophical references, prompted me to look back on my life, to look around me as I lived (I was in prison after all) and to look into the future. It allowed me to continue on to law school, to two graduate schools, to teaching in universities, to developing and directing social programs, to teaching and traveling in Europe and Asia and now on to this book. It was a process that provided a perspective on America that remains as powerful now as it did when I opened that first book in my cell.

So, this book is about this process and what it made me think about, see and do, and what it's led me to become. There is certainly a point to the book. But, at the same time, there is a story told, about someone born into the almost unparalleled time of 1950's America, someone who got into prison, got out and then got on. It's a review of the myriad of experiences I've been fortunate enough to have, of the assortments of people and places I've encountered and of the observations I've made along the way. It's about all these things—things that support *The Making of an American Social Thinker.*

With the review of the "why" and "what," I must say something about the "almost didn't." I had a great deal of difficulty with this book, particularly in getting it organized. Despite many attempts, using a variety of methods, I could not assemble my thoughts or even find a point from which to begin. After throwing hundreds of pages away, I was very close to giving up. Then my long-time friend, Phil Pisani, came into the picture. Phil and I share many things. We grew up together, so we share a sense of neighborhood as well as a sense of what it was like in post-WWII America. Phil is also an ex-felon, stemming from a gambling conviction in his younger years. He now possesses a master's degree in public administration and policy analysis and, in addition to being a respected family man, is a labor investigator for the Department of Labor in New York. Phil also writes screenplays which, given his understanding of the writing process, helped a great deal with getting this book off the ground. Finally, Phil felt a book of this type had value, providing me with the inspiration I needed. In short, my old pal Phil was an essential part of this book.

So, here it is, a book written about experiences supportive of the appellation "American Social Thinker," intended to create dialogue on what is happening in America. We believe it is a book for everyone, other social thinkers, other academics and other people interested in the American "experiment."

Part One begins the story of how I ended up in prison. Setting the stage for the period in my life when I began to take things on a much more serious note, it is a hodgepodge of information woven together without importance placed on sequence. Although we were a bit apprehensive that this skipping around might cause some confusion for the reader, we decided that, given the amount of information we had to mention, about my crime, my lifestyle, my past, my family and my thoughts as incarceration began, we would stick with how the pieces naturally came to us.

Part One also deals with my prison experience. It references a time when many things were happening to me and around me. It was a time when my academic program, filled with theories related to politics and economics and especially crime was developed, came head-to-head with the practicalities of my being a criminal in prison. In short, it was a time that would serve as the basis for my continuing concern about the world in which we live.

Part Two focuses on my release from prison, some of the circumstances that held me in balance and some that tried to tip me back to my criminal ways. It tells of my continuation with academics and the beginnings of my professional career. It recalls a time of serious considerations, a time when I began to actively challenge our American process.

Part Three reviews the development of my teaching career as well as my more extensive involvement with social problems and social programs. It covers a time when, given what I was teaching, and simultaneously working at in the community, I felt almost driven out of the country.

Part Four talks about my leaving the United States, and my experiences with teaching and traveling in Europe and Asia. This chapter provides information about how I began to see our country from afar, what I learned about how those in other parts of the world view us and how I began to review and re-think some of my ideas. It also talks about my decision to return stateside.

Part Five represents the conclusion of the book, recognizing that it is far from conclusive. My hope is that, at this point, readers will be convinced of the "American Social Thinker" credit, as they are encouraged to consider all the faces, places and the variety of circumstances, situations and information that have crossed my life's path.

This should, in turn, provide support for the assumptions made in the book. These assumptions will be reviewed and will point to where I believe the major struggles lie for our society, and to how this book can help contribute to the development of a dialogue from which we can better understand these struggles.

In the end, I hope the readers will see themselves within the context of what they read. I hope the book will help them see themselves and others through life experiences, political and economic variables and history, recognizing that they in their own right can and should be "social thinkers," capable of contributing in meaningful ways to America's next century.

PART ONE

If you want knowledge, you must take part in the practice of changing reality. If you want to know the taste of a pear, you must change the pear by eating it yourself...All genuine knowledge originates in direct experience.

- Mao -

Chapter 1

JAIL

It was the beginning of my second week in the Clark County Jail, Las Vegas, Nevada, 1977. It was midday and I knew it was a gray one as I caught a glimpse from the only window accessible to us inmates. It was a long strip of a window running along the wall of a hallway that ran from the cellblocks to the chow hall. As we were herded toward mealtime, most everyone had a tendency to linger in this hallway a bit, trying to get a sense of the sun, the rain, the wind or whatever. It was our connection to the outside world and as we gazed it conjured up in us particular visions of freedom.

I remember wanting to jump through the glass, to the sidewalk two stories below, to become part of the traffic, to feel my feet going in any direction I wanted them to go, just to participate in the daily coming and going. But it was only a moment's respite as fellow inmates or the guards would prompt the line along its route, beyond the window and into the noisy, yellowed-from-age, sour-smelling chow hall. The jailhouse mindset would quickly return in a lot less time than it took to describe our revelry. It's a mindset of anger, mixed with despair, covered over with some form of bravado. And it creates a feeling that shoots out to those around you, to those controlling you, to those free on the outside and, ultimately, right back to its source. Perpetrators...victims...pain...anger...the lines of who's who and what's what are fuzzy to begin with. And in here, they become as blurry as they can be. Confinement, the loss of liberty...make no mistake about them. They do create desperate places. And the starch that I was now staring at on my plate only added to the desperation.

I was on the fourth floor of the county jail, where the more serious criminals were held. Included here were individuals, like myself, who had been sentenced to longer times (about 10 years or more) and who were waiting transport to actual prison. Also housed on this floor were those who had been sent from prison to the jail because of some pending legal action, most likely a hearing on another crime they had committed while in prison. (The public gets a bit confused, but there are differences between jails and prisons, the most general being that jails are short-term facilities, holding people, usually the "lighter end" offender, for shorter periods of time.)

My floor was made up of two rows of cells, each facing the other. There was a walkway dividing the two rows, allowing the guards to check on the inmates. There was a set of bars running on both sides of the walkway, and in between those bars and the actual cell bars was another walkway, which allowed the inmates some room to walk when the cells were open. There were generally two individuals to a cell, but when the place got crowded, particularly on weekends, you could expect several other guests to arrive. "Cadillac Row" was just down the "tier"(walkway) from my cell. It was so named because the cement floor always had a polish on it, primarily because those housed in the cells were the most violent and dangerous in the place. I guess it was this jail's equivalent of the reserved section at the racetrack or the special tables at your finer eateries.

As did the other inmates, I often hung out in front of my cell, smoking cigarettes, gazing down the tier at the constantly flickering TV stuck on the wall, mumbling with the other inmates as they passed by. I had a million thoughts running through my head, mostly directed at what I was going to do with myself for the next several years. You could spend some time thinking about things like this, but the noise of the place—inmates yelling at each other over card games, cigarettes, sex or whatever, the bars clanging, the TV, everything sort of bouncing off the walls—made it difficult to concentrate. You could also try to read, which I did, or write, which I did, or listen to the stories which ran through the cells, which I tried not to do. Most of them were filled with exaggeration about crimes, women or fighting, and sometimes all three. Most of them were laughable. The others were pathetic.

But I was interested in one man's story, that of Jesse B. He was the most notable of the Cadillac Row group, a convicted killer facing the death penalty, and he was in the jail, down from the prison, awaiting another disposition hearing on his sentence. I had never met anyone in that situation and I was interested in knowing exactly what he was thinking about at this juncture. It was several days, and a dozen or so nods in passing, before we actually spoke. It was and is part of the ritual (both inside and out by the way), for anyone who "knows," to approach things this way. Faces become acquaintances and acquaintances friends via this ritual. And so it went.

As we moved from the nods and then the "hey, man" to actual conversation, I found out that Jesse was not holding to any form of innocence for the murder he committed. Quite the contrary, he admitted to being the murderous type and he was willing to pay the price. His logic, which was to become more important to me years later as I argued the "humanness" of the death penalty, was simple, but by no means conventional. He told me that he felt no remorse for the things he had done, and that this "non-feeling" came from what he described as a lack of attachment to morality. He wasn't sure why he had this anti-social characteristic, but he knew he had it and he felt that this didn't give him a fitting place in society. He therefore reasoned that if he were put to death he might find himself on a better plane of existence than the one he was currently on. And so, he really didn't have an objection to, nor an impending fear of, execution.

It seemed however, that Jesse's position was being challenged by his lawyers, who were trying to convince him that if he stayed alive (i.e. if he could get a "life without possibility of parole" sentence in lieu of the death sentence) he could then write a book, from which a movie deal was already being discussed, and give the proceeds to the victim's family. And this was why he was here, in county jail, as his lawyers tried to negotiate their views, and probably their money interests, relative to what Jesse deserved. So there we were, a heroin dealer and a murderer, blowing the smoke from our Camels, taking stabs at the "fucked-up criminal justice system," talking about life and wondering about death. Truly a jail experience to remember. I never talked with him after these days, as he surely struggled with his thoughts. But Jesse B. was executed in late 1979, so I guess he won out over his lawyers' plea.

What eventually happened, I knew was coming. It was something I thought about on a daily basis but would manage to put aside for the sake of my more immediate pleasures. The police had been on my trail for awhile, but the lifestyle of a drug "racketeer," particularly in Las Vegas, particularly for someone who was only twenty-five years old living out a boyhood dream, clouded the concerns I might have had. I was becoming a "somebody" in town. I was getting to know the "right" people, the "right" places and how and where to spend my money. I drove a new, dark blue, Fleetwood Cadillac with my initials on the plates. I wore expensive clothes in the best of gangster taste as well as gold jewelry reworked by a "fence" who only a few people knew about. I played golf almost everyday, relaxed by the pool and gambled at the tables and on sporting events as I pleased. I spent a lot of time in bars, particularly my "hang-out," where I would drink with my Mexican-American partners while discussing life, leisure and business. And several times a month I would take a trip, for buying or selling purposes, a trip punctuated by more bars, more women and more "fun." And to top it all off, I had a pretty girlfriend who lived with me in a quiet, residential, townhouse village, where neighbors were friendly but kept their distance.

Life at this time, then, was not hard to take. It had not always been this way and I actually considered myself fortunate to be in the position I was in. It made me feel successful when people from my hometown in New York, who would come to Vegas on gambling junkets, could see how I lived. I knew they were returning home with the word, "Hey, Jimmy P. is making it happen!" And, to some extent, I was. The fact that my lifestyle was supported by the drug business, a business that had severe consequences for all involved, was not of particular concern.

When I did have my guilty moments, and they did come, I would brush them away with a dose of my own medicine. I could also rationalize that I was what I was, no worse than your average business man, cramming things down people's throats that they didn't need and couldn't afford. No worse than your average lawyer or politician, lying every time their lips moved. No worse, maybe even better.

My house of cards came tumbling down one late fall afternoon. A security guard who worked for our complex came to my door to inform me that someone was "playing around" with my Cadillac. He wasn't sure that any mischief was taking place, but he felt I should be notified of such incidents. I had been readying myself for a shower, and with only a towel about, I asked my girlfriend to go with him to check out what was going on. Within minutes of their departure I heard some commotion at my door and, still in towel, I walked toward it to see what the problem was.

As I approached the door, it burst open and five men poured into my place, guns drawn, identifying themselves as drug agents, and yelling "FREEZE" and "DON'T MOVE." I immediately recognized one of the agents as a man I had been doing some business with, and I saw in his undercover-agent eyes a taunting look—a look that showed that these men would like nothing better than if I decided not to heed their warning. I tried not to move a muscle as they twisted the handcuffs onto my wrists.

I watched as they began their "show," tossing things about, talking tough, asking questions without waiting for or even caring about responses, puffing and buffing as they made their way through an initial search of the place. They were looking for drugs or guns or anything else they could find that might add to their case. They were trying to unnerve me, to get me to say things about my partners, to make me realize that I was now their property, and that this was only the beginning of my problems. They were doing their job, and they were doing it well. They continued the search, but what they really wanted they knew they already had.

My arrest came on the tail of a secret grand jury indictment, a process where the state presents evidence to a jury, seeking an indictment, prior to one's arrest. It was the result of a year-long investigation into my drug activity. The police had been tipped to my business by a person who, seeking to escape from his own problems with the law, had told them he had gotten drugs from someone, who was working for someone else, who was a major player in the drug scene in Vegas. This person introduced a drug agent to that first someone who did work for me and who also happened to be my girlfriend's brother. My girlfriend's brother then unsuspectingly introduced the drug agent to my girlfriend on a day when all three just happened to meet while shopping at a Vegas mall. They chatted a bit that afternoon, and as they were leaving, the undercover agent noticed that the parking valet brought around to my girlfriend a new, dark blue, Fleetwood Cadillac with my initials inscribed on the plates. He, of course, followed up on this lead, and there I was, a person who had now became a focus of drug-related investigations.

As part of these investigations the agent then told my girlfriend's brother that he was, in fact, significantly involved in the cocaine business in Denver, and that he and his partners might be interested in exchanging pounds of coke for pounds of heroin if the right connection could be made. He suggested that my girlfriend's brother put him in touch with "the man" to see if there was an interest in this type transaction. When I was told about this possibility I was indeed interested. I had already recognized that coke was fast becoming the drug of choice in the U.S. and that it was being sold at prices far above its actual value. Yet, I hesitated at first, primarily because my main partner (a man of Mexican descent whose family had been in the heroin trade for generations and a man I genuinely liked and respected) thought that the "girl"(a slang term used for coke as opposed to "boy" for heroin) would only bring trouble. But the possibility of expanding into a more lucrative market made me greedy, and I decided to at least talk with this man.

My girlfriend met with her brother's acquaintance initially, as they had already been introduced, to feel out what kind of fellow he actually was. She seemed to think he was a good guy and she even sold him some of our "private stock," without any reprisal. He and I then met on several occasions, and he portrayed himself as another Italian boy, someone much like myself, someone just trying to catch a piece of the good life. We did drugs together --usually the test to see if one is actually a cop--and I did provide him with several samples of my goods. We talked about making a lot of money, but nothing actually materialized. Perhaps it was because he could not get beyond me to any of my other partners, or perhaps it was because he thought they had enough on me and the police could get to my partners through the pressures of my arrest. Whatever the reason, as this "nothing" occurred, I began to sense that this man was a cop, and that I was probably in deep trouble. I cut off my contact with him but it was already too late. The evidence of this fact I was now watching unfold, as I sat, handcuffed and toweled, on my living room sofa.

My girlfriend and I were taken from the house to county jail. She was also indicted as was her brother, although I knew that this trouble belonged to me. We were separated there as I was booked, fingerprinted, roughed up a bit and put into a large holding cell with about seven other men who appeared to be mostly drunks and vagrants. The night passed with all kinds of thoughts running through my brain, some lingering for a moment only to be pushed out by others. How had I gotten to this point? What would happen next? What would happen to my girlfriend and her brother? Who did the cops think they were? What kind of people are they anyway? What kind of person was I? What would my mother think of me?

My only distraction to these questions came from watching one of my cellmates who was "drying out." He would occasionally pull his penis out and guide it into the partially open mouth of a chubby, black youngster who was passed out on one of the cell's benches. The youngster would wake up, fend off the assault almost as if not recognizing what was actually happening, and then pass out again. The same cycle would then occur. It was the type of grotesque and disgusting, yet absurdly humorous behavior, that I would become all too familiar with during the years ahead. Fortunately, for the moment, I was spared more of the drama, as my girlfriend, her brother and I were bailed out the following day.

It was a night whose image remains vivid in my mind. It was about 10 p.m., and I was standing in a corridor looking through a doorway. The door was open enough for me to see my attorney, feet propped up on his desk, one hand to the forehead while the other held a document which he was reading intensely. As I entered the dimly lit room I could see that his face had a look of deep concern. I was in for some bad news.

Steve, my lawyer, had phoned me earlier, asking that I come to his office as soon as possible. He had just received my pre-sentence report and we needed to talk about its content. The pre-sentence report, which he now held in his hands, was a document reviewing an interview I had been through with the Department of Parole and Probation. The purpose of the report was to provide to the court, via an analysis of my interview and other information pertinent to the charges against me, a recommendation as to what type of sentence the court should consider meting out.

My lawyer and I figured that the recommendation would be on the lighter end of the scale. Granted, I was involved in the drug business. This certainly carried with it, especially with the drug being heroin, assumptions as to one's involvement in other anti-social behavior. And the police seemed to be convinced, more by innuendo than real proof, that I was a member of the largest narcotics operation in the West. Furthermore, I had refused to cooperate with their advances in terms of "giving up" other people in exchange for leniency. Yet, and I know this sounds strange and contradictory, I liked to think of myself as a good guy, someone who was fair, who supplied people with "clean" drugs, who never cheated people out of their money. Someone who never went out of his way to harm others, who even counseled those who were drugging themselves into oblivion and someone who, with principle in mind, never put anyone "next" to the police. I was, in street sense, a "straight shooter." More importantly, I had only minor scrapes with the law in the past, having no prior felony arrests or convictions.

I also expressed to the Department of Parole and Probation interviewer that I was willing to own up to what I had done, that I would plead guilty to the two sale of heroin charges against me and take responsibility for involving my girlfriend and her brother with my activities. Additionally, I presented the interviewer with a plan, one that involved me going to college while working in the community, instead of going to prison. I suggested to her how this plan of probation could be held over my head. If I didn't conform to it, I could then be sent to prison. I reasoned with her that this would provide me with a chance for redemption, while simultaneously giving the Department of Parole and Probation the chance to still meet its objectives.

Given the pros and cons, Steve and I estimated that the balance should be tipped in my favor. We felt that a minimum stay in prison might be forthcoming, but we hoped that some form of probation would be the recommendation.

As Steve handed me the pre-sentence report, I was surprised by its thickness. I quickly leafed through it to the final page where I knew the recommendation could be found. I understood why Steve had such a look of concern on his face as what I read hit me like a heavyweight's left. On each of the two sale counts, the recommendation was the maximum sentence allowable under the law, 20 years in prison. Furthermore, it was suggested that the two sentences run consecutively versus concurrently, where both sentences run simultaneously. This meant that I would finish one of the 20-year sentences and then go on to the next one.

Steve quickly pointed out that in the complicated parlance of sentencing schemes this didn't mean a straight 40 years. Rather, in Nevada, this translated into the following: I would do approximately five years on the first offense (a quarter of sentence) and then I would be eligible for parole. If I received a parole, of which there is absolutely no guarantee, I would then go on to do a minimum of another five years on the second count, and then be eligible (only "eligible") for a parole which would then get me out of prison. In other words, I would do a minimum of 10 years in prison, with the possibility, more likely the likelihood, of doing more.

I wasn't prepared for these numbers and I was angry. I cleared Steve's desk with a sweep of my hand, yelling profanities and accusing him of being an overpriced and worthless "piece of shit." He had assured me throughout that prison time, if I were to get any at all, would be minimal. He had said that he was affiliated with the most prestigious firm in the state, and he knew his way around the block, and, and... Things flashed across my mind about some of his advice, like when he had asked me at one of my hearings if I was a heavy user of heroin. I replied that I was only a recreational user, getting high on occasion. His advice was that I try "shooting up" more regularly so I could evidence some track marks. This "drug addict" image, he so lawyerly opined, might elicit more sympathy from the court, compared to the image of a cold, "only in it for the money," profiteer, increasing my chances for leniency.

It took me several minutes to calm down. By then I could see that Steve, although frightened, was honestly upset with what had happened. He suggested I sit and read the entire report as what he had read raised some doubts in his mind. I read through the report in more detail and I could clearly see what Steve was referring to. There were allegations of my involvement with drug activity in Las Vegas prior to my ever being in Nevada. There were unsubstantiated references to drug contacts in other parts of the world that I knew nothing about. There were remarks about the type of car I drove, my lifestyle and my attitude, all in a manner that would connote "wise-guy." In addition, there was a heavy accent on my crimes, and even more on the fact that I would not cooperate with the police in providing information about my associates. This is one of the many twists in the criminal justice system—honoring deceit while chastising integrity. There was little mention of the honesty with which I approached the interview, my desire to accept responsibility for the involvement of my girlfriend and her brother or my plan for rehabilitation. In short, the report was clearly biased.

We sat and discussed our concerns about the misleading and untrue statements in the report, and about its overall tone. Steve then offered a suggestion that made me think of him as the good lawyer that he actually was. He said that he would telephone the judge that was presiding over my case, a man he knew very well from a variety of social and professional affiliations, and the man who would ultimately be responsible for deciding on my sentence. He would explain the discrepancies in the report to the judge and ask him for some type of reconsideration in light of the circumstances. Steve felt that we would surely get some type of positive reaction from the judge.

The following day I received a phone call from Steve telling me that he did indeed have positive news, as well as an interesting story, and that I should come to his office as soon as possible. Within an hour's time I was sitting in his office listening to what was a rather bewildering tale. Steve had been a bit suspicious about the outcome of the report, especially since I had had such good feelings about the interview process. In investigating what might have gone wrong he made an important discovery. It seemed that the woman who had conducted the interview and written the report was romantically linked to one of the primary agents responsible for my arrest. This link then, could very well have been the reason for the tenor of the report. To the point, it appeared the report was more a review of what the agent/police thought of me rather than one that reflected what she and I had discussed.

Steve had already talked with the judge about the report and the ethical dilemma as well. The judge, recognizing a problem, was willing to tender an offer. If I would plead guilty to both charges, he would agree to sentence me to 10 years in prison on the first charge, with 20 years probation on the second, the second running concurrent with the first. This meant, and bear with me on this one, that, as to the first, 10-year prison sentence, I would serve a minimum of two to two-and-one-half years in prison before I became eligible for parole, at which time I could get released to serve the remainder of my time on parole. As to the second, concurrent sentence, this meant I would be on probation (usually implying that you serve your time in the community) while in prison, and also for a time if and when I got out. Therefore, while I was doing my prison time, I would be subject to certain rules of probationary behavior, particularly "not getting into any trouble." If I violated these rules my probationary status would be revoked and the 20-year concurrent probation sentence would become a 20-year consecutive prison sentence. In other words, should I mess-up while in prison (not necessarily being found guilty of an actual criminal offense) I would be subject to being paroled from the first 10-year prison sentence directly into a second 20-year prison sentence.

The judge was using what was commonly referred to as creative sentencing, giving me the possibility for less time should I keep my nose clean or more time should I not. He was also ensuring that the authorities had as much leverage as possible to control my behavior should I consider continuing on a criminal path, like being involved in drug activity from within prison. The judge also said that he would include in this offer a recommendation to the judge handling the cases for my girlfriend and her brother that both receive probation in light of my accepting to go to prison. He made it clear to Steve that, should I not like this deal, he would send the report back to the Department of Parole and Probation and, noting the previous problems, ask for another one to be done. He would then accept, on this second turn, whatever they might recommend. The judge told Steve he expected an answer that day.

I reviewed the options. I was not happy with going to prison for two to three years and then relying on a parole board to get out. Parole boards can be very selective, denying parole simply on the basis that one should do more time on the crimes committed. But it was less time than originally recommended, and my girlfriend and her brother would be treated leniently. Moreover, if the report was sent back to Parole and Probation, particularly with the "rap" of allowing unethical activity to occur, I could bet on it coming back with the same maximum recommendation as before.

I considered simply pleading not guilty as this would delay any decisions I had to make. But the evidence against me was strong, and I stood a very good chance of being found guilty at trial. And if this occurred, the same judge, who had already offered me the chance to avoid all this bother and to help with "the girlfriend and her brother" situation, would undoubtedly respond with the maximum sentence. It appeared I had no other choice. Besides...I knew I was guilty. (I did consider running away, most likely to Mexico, but the thought of being a fugitive for the rest of my life wasn't all that entertaining either.)

I asked Steve what he thought. His feelings were that it would be better to put closure to the situation, as it could drag on for more time than I would probably spend in prison, with the chance of even more drastic results should I not accept the current offer. He also said that he would do all that he possibly could to help me with things I might need in prison, as well as with parole board considerations when that time arrived. Attempting to bolster my spirits he also said, with a pat on the back, that a few years in prison wouldn't be any problem for a guy like me. I smiled back at him, acknowledging his input, but more marveling at what pieces of work lawyers can be.

During the next few days we formalized the terms for my guilty plea. Within a week I was standing in court, dressed in my most conservative suit, with my toothbrush in my pocket. I knew I was "going away." I was in front of the judge who had already agreed to the plea but who, because such negotiations aren't considered proper "for the record," insisted that I act like I was hearing my 10-year prison and 20-year concurrent probation sentence for the first time. It all took about 20 minutes, after which I was handcuffed and put into the custody of the Clark County Jail. My sentence was beginning.

Jesse B. was interesting indeed, but his situation provided more of a distraction than anything, a distraction from the thoughts about myself and what I had done. Depression hit quickly and solidly, the kind that manifests itself from the perceptions of failure. I was seeing myself as someone who had been given more than adequate individual abilities, someone who had been born into a family that provided every opportunity to constructively develop those abilities and someone who had managed to abuse both to the point of shame.

My parents were hardworking people. They had struggled through poor childhood, and as young adults, through the depression. My father, like so many others, was in and out of work. But, just prior to his soldiering in Europe during WWII, he was, after asking the president of the company for work, able to land a job with a developing company in our hometown called International Business Machines, more commonly known as I.B.M. My mother took his job during the war years, and when my father returned, they began to have children and raise a family.

The job, the family, the house...they took their responsibilities with utmost concern, raising my sister and me with love, care and pride. We went to church as a family, we had nice clothes and we were taught to be polite and respectful. We belonged to the I.B.M. Country Club, a splendid place with golf courses, bowling alleys, tennis courts, baseball fields, swimming pools, billiard rooms, a library, and a huge gymnasium, all of which were surrounded by areas for picnics and family outings. The company built the facility with a focus on family recreation and it offered to its employees the chance to experience leisure in ways that would have otherwise been impossible. It certainly gave me the opportunity to participate in all of the junior sport leagues there, and I became a good athlete because of it.

I had the ideal older sister, who was kind to me and who helped me learn, me often playing student to her teacher. We had many relatives, and I was always surrounded by aunts and uncles who seemed to take favor with me. I had all these fine people and fine things around me, people and things which spoke to the potential of my developing character.

I could recall how bright I had been in my school years. In the primary grades it was suggested to my parents that I be advanced a grade since I was learning at a faster pace than my peers. At the age of eleven I was even allowed to tutor other kids who were falling behind with their schoolwork. In junior high school I became part of an advanced program, a group of about 20 kids who were taught higher-level classes, including a then-progressive course in a foreign language. In high school, I continued with the advanced classes, and with hardly any study I finished in the top fifth of my class.

However, it seemed that despite my academic potential and my athletic and social skills, I chose to apply my abilities in a different direction—a direction shaded by its connection to semi-legitimate and illegitimate endeavors. In short, I became good at "hustling" money. I learned how to play cards and shoot pool well. I caddied at our local private golf club and I would play golf for money on our Monday caddies' day. I had the most lucrative paper route in town, dotted with neighborhood bars and restaurants and barber shops and grocery stores. These were the places that tended to give the best tips to their carrier, and, given the nature of the area of town I grew up in, the best chances to pick up a few extra bucks for favors done. It was probably this factor—my part of town, my neighborhood—that had the greatest influence on where I was now situated.

In addition to having the large corporate presence of an I.B.M., my town in upstate New York was also strongly influenced by organized crime. This was particularly true of my north side neighborhood, the Italian section of town. Everyone there seemed to have a connection to the local crime "syndicate." It was an integral, as well as accepted, part of our community. As a kid in my early teens I was fascinated with this world, the stories, the lifestyles, the money. And my paper route took me directly to the most important hang-outs for the "fellas" I so admired. I would pick up little jobs on my route, running information from one place to another, always gathering up some extra "tip" money for my work. It was a great feeling for a kid. I made good money and, just as important, I was known by the older men as someone who could be trusted.

We also had our gang, a version of a fraternity with initiation rights and all, and it parroted the activities of the adult crime organization. We weren't, however, considered bad kids by those in the neighborhood. In fact, a good number of the guys involved in our club stayed away from any seriously consequential behavior. But some of us did hang out on the corner, and some of us did get into fights, and some of us did impose ourselves on others, and some of us did get into serious trouble. For us, the fact that we created fear in other people represented an important sense of power. And the fact that we could operate under the shield of organized crime, with our run-ins with the law usually handled via neighborhood "connections," only lent credibility to this power. It was in our eyes a truly enviable situation. We could make girls, we could make money and we could make fun. In our minds what more could anyone want?

The same mindset carried over to the state university I attended in northern New York. I hardly ever attended classes there, but I did become involved in gambling and the developing drug business. I became a local celebrity of sorts, making and spending money in the local taverns, fraternizing with the owners as well as with all the college women. It was fun and exciting and I convinced myself that somehow, in these type activities, I had found my calling. I was good at being a wise-guy. I never really considered the merit of using my abilities in any other way. And as I traveled on to Miami, then back to New York and then on to Las Vegas, I couldn't even imagine why I should.

But now I was in county jail and I was thinking otherwise. I was a convicted heroin dealer, a person who had, no doubt, hurt others. I was someone who had abused his own potential and let his family down. And I was on my way to the penitentiary. I shook my head at the feelings of disbelief and disgust. There would be much more to think about in the time ahead, a puzzle of hows and whys for sure. And there was certainly my new environment to contend with. But I knew that I was fortunate. I still had possession of the abilities I had until now abused, abilities given to me by another source that I had wrongly credited to my own being. I was now hoping, no I was making a pact with myself, that through whatever lie ahead, I would make my time pay off. I would put my abilities to proper use, somehow get a college education and redeem myself with it. It was time to move on, and, as the ironies of life often are, it was in this kind of place, in jail, that I felt the spirit to make it happen.

Chapter 2

PRISON

"Palombo, roll 'em-up!" The early morning call from a guard echoed through the cell block. I was going somewhere. I took my state-allocated bed mat and towel, rolled them up together and prepared myself to leave the jail. This had happened to me before, when I was transferred to the city jail from the county, but the change lasted less than a day and I was returned to the county facility. Why this had occurred was never explained, but bureaucratic miscommunication or simple dim-wittedness were two likely bets. So I wasn't exactly sure what was going on in this instance.

The double row of bars was opened and I was escorted to the small room where inmate personal items were stored. The officer behind the counter handed me the suit, shoes, shirt and tie I had worn at my sentencing as well as my watch, ring and dark glasses. As I signed the receipt for the items, he told me to get dressed and be seated. I was then to wait for further instructions.

I enjoyed getting out of the jail coveralls, putting on my custom made white shirt and gray, silk-blend suit. My black calfskin shoes felt great on my feet as I laid the band of my gold watch over my wrist and placed my 18 kt. gold signet ring on my little finger. I looped my black silk tie around my neck and put my dark glasses on. I sensed the rush of getting "cleaned-up."

I felt like a million bucks, and the guard's covetous reaction to the transition pumped my adrenaline even more. But, within a moment's time, I was in a curious state of being, a state with which I wasn't all that familiar. I could definitely detect that my inside was different than my outside--the one simply didn't match the other! I actually became a bit uncomfortable as I realized that perhaps my Vegas image was fading as fast as my Vegas tan.

My thoughts were interrupted by a short, slightly-built Mexican American inmate who entered the room and began the process I had just completed. His clothes were a bit worn, but he snapped on the lapels of his plaid polyester sport coat with the same "I feel like a million bucks" attitude I had displayed. He tried to joke with the guard behind the counter, turning to me with quick glances for reinforcement of his humor. But he wasn't very funny. He was however a friendly sort, and we lit up a smoke and engaged in some idle conversation. His name was Bennie and he was a bit nervous, really wondering about where we were going. I was also curious, but kept the face of someone who might know the answer. As we chatted I would see him measuring my attitude as well as my attire... it was clear he was thinking that I was someone who might be worth knowing. Before our conversation developed, two guards walked into the room and informed us that we were going on a trip. As we were made ready with handcuffs and leg irons, Bennie and I could only figure that we were headed for northern Nevada, to the maximum security prison in Carson City.

Generally, inmates were transported north via bus in larger groups escorted by four or five guards, so we couldn't be sure what was happening. We were placed in a van and, much to our surprise, taken to the airport where we boarded the private, twin-engine plane used to transport state officials. We were indeed headed for the northern facility, but in a manner that no one could have anticipated. Bennie was convinced that this preferential treatment had something to do with his elegantly dressed traveling companion, but I simply shrugged my shoulders as he incessantly asked how all this came about. Although I was also unsure, and to this day can't explain it, my "street sense" told me that remaining quiet would best suit the situation. I did think, however, that this style of travel sure was a lucky break.

On arrival, we were escorted through the airport terminal, handcuffs and leg irons in place. I remember gazing at people who were walking about, going and coming, moving freely. I thought about how great it was to travel and how great it would be to be like them. Everyone noticed us, passing with varying degrees of caution and disdain. One little boy came up to me and stared into my dark glasses with a look of wonderment. Perhaps, this was his first opportunity to see a "real" criminal. I smiled back at him as a woman quickly grabbed his hand and whisked him off in that scolding mother's way. I didn't like the way this all made me feel, but I had other things to think about as we moved out of the airport.

Bennie and I were put into an official vehicle that would take us to the prison. Although I clung to my stoicism I was becoming edgy and nervous. We were going to the penitentiary, the "big house," and although it promised relief from the limited confines of the jail, it was not a place I had ever been. We drove a few miles and then turned into a road leading to the prison. It was beginning to get dark. Through the dimness I saw the gate, and the walls, and the guard towers and the buildings...stone...gray...old. The coldness of it all hit me. I was honestly afraid. This was a place one should never want to be.

Bennie was in an even more heightened state of nervousness as we were brought into the main holding area. I was trying to numb myself to the surroundings, and at the same time I kept thinking about my parents, my family and myself. Education kept popping into my head. I'll get into it, I'll learn, I'll get my degree, I'll not waste the years in here, I'll turn this all around and become something. I'll become something more than what this place was suggesting...something more than what that little boy at the airport had seen. I must do it.

For the first 30 days, all new inmates are held in the "fish tank." This is a portion of the prison where the incoming are initially diagnosed. Each inmate is given a cell which is actually like a small room with a heavy metal door, and for most of the day that is where he stays. It is a time for prison officials to observe the inmates (like fish in a bowl), to administer medical and psychological tests, to have the inmate speak with the chaplain and with a counselor, and to ascertain if there are any enemies in the general population who might cause the inmate harm or find out if the inmate might have the idea of harming someone else. Boot-camp style haircuts are given, showers are allowed once a day and three meals are delivered to each cell by cart. Advice is given about how to get along in prison, and everyone is drilled on the rules and regulations and how the administration and guard staff operate. Inmate programs are explained and the inmates are cautioned as to what type activities to avoid, especially the gang-related type.

A good portion of my days were spent in isolation and I thought a great deal about "doing" my time. I wasn't exactly sure what to expect out there "on the yard," but I realized I would have to be very careful with whom I associated, with what I said and with what I did. I would have to be very cautious with all aspects of my behavior, staying alert to both the inmates and the guards around me. I would have to pace myself as I got integrated into this community, a community where I would be spending a great deal of monotonous time-day-to-day, week-to-week, month-to-month, year-to-year. It was not going to be easy, but then again, it wasn't supposed to be.

Late every night my thoughts would turn to prayer, to a God whose image was unclear to me, but who I hoped could help. I prayed for help in keeping myself and my family healthy, and for help with the development of an education program from which I could turn my life around. I would pray to the point of crying. These were deep, soul-searching and often hurtful moments. But as I received the first letters from my family--my parents, my sister and my uncles and aunts--all encouraging me with their love and hope, I recognized how blessed I already was. I wasn't sure how this "prayer-to-God-to-inspiration" worked, but I had no doubt that I could feel it working.

One morning, while in the fish tank, I was due to have my blood drawn for testing. As my cell door was opened I was surprised to see that the doctor's assistant sent in to administer the procedure was an old acquaintance of mine named Sam. Sam and I knew each other from the drug business in Vegas. When I first met him he had been a fairly important dealer, but he eventually fell into the ever-present trap of becoming addicted to his product. He lost most of what he had obtained from the business--his car, his house, his status--as the hectic and treacherous world of the addict took its toll. It was through the twists and turns of that world, he told me, that he ended up in prison. He had been "in" for about six months and being a doctor's assistant was his new job. We talked a bit about the outside and people we knew. I recalled the time that Sam had sold me a new TV and video set he had come by in one of his deals. But after finding out from another associate that Sam had actually stolen the items from his mother's house while she was vacationing in order to get money for his overpowering drug habit, I insisted on its return. I let him keep the money, and I even helped him bring the set back to his mother's house. All the while we joked about how difficult it would be to explain to any passing police officer that we were actually returning the goods and not stealing them. It was a pathetic story by all accounts, but we now chuckled at the memory nonetheless.

Sam returned a few days later with some preliminary results, but his primary reason for the visit was to let me know that another friend of mine, an old buddy from my neighborhood in New York was also a "guest" at the prison. He told me that Joe, or Jughead as we used to call him back in our younger days because he kept getting himself into foolish predicaments, had been there for about three months and that he had told Joe I was "in town." Sam told me that Joe had fallen in with the right people during his stay and that he was looking forward to seeing me and to introducing me to his new friends. As I heard this, I felt a sense of relief. I knew Joe well, both from our neighborhood and Vegas. We had actually lived together when I first arrived in town, and he introduced me to a number of people, particularly women, whom I became friends with. Joe also worked with me in Vegas, as he bought drugs from my business and fenced stolen goods with my associates. And occasionally, when he found himself in one of those predicaments he was famous for, or simply short of gambling cash, I would give him a few bucks to help.

So, now I knew I had a connection, a paisan, an old neighbor pal. I had someone whom I could trust, someone who respected me and someone who had already made a way with the "right" people. It relaxed me a bit to know this, and I had a smile on face when I began to hear a voice through my cell window, coming from out on the yard, yelling, "Hey Jimmy...see ya soon!"

Other things were occurring while I was in the fish tank. My interview with the prison chaplain provided me with several pieces of important information. While discussing my interest in participating in an education program, he encouraged me to take my time with the educational and psychological tests that would be administered. It appeared that most inmates took them as a matter of routine, not really paying attention to the ramifications of the outcome. He made it clear to me that I should not let this happen. "Jim," he said, "almost all the people working in this place will not believe you. They will doubt your word from the beginning and you will have to prove to them otherwise. How you respond to the tests will provide the administration with information that will be important to your future here. Be careful with those tests!" This advice blended well with my own thoughts on how I should proceed with my initial period of incarceration--stay aware and be careful.

The chaplain had more to say, but it was not all encouraging. He informed me that, to the best of his knowledge, the Nevada Prison System did not provide an education program that would allow me to accomplish my goals of obtaining a four-year university degree. To his recollection, there was a junior college program offered to "lifers" (those serving life sentences) but the program was available generally after these types had served a minimum of five years, in a sort of "proving your worth" period. This didn't match at all with my intentions, as I was neither a lifer, nor did I anticipate spending five years in the facility to prove my worth. Nor did I need but a few junior college courses. In spite of my involvement with drugs, drinking and gambling, I did obtain credit for a number of freshman and sophomore courses while I was enrolled in college in New York.

This news threw me a curve. It never occurred to me that a prison system would not provide the possibility for an average inmate to pursue a college degree. But the chaplain was sitting across from me telling me that this was the case. And when I asked what the chances were for developing such a program, his response relating the nature of prison bureaucracy, the accompanying punishment-oriented mindset, the lack of any real demand for a program of this sort and the lack of funds even if a demand were present, all translated into slim and none. However, I should not lose hope, he encouraged.

I should do my best, in whatever fashion, to read, write and learn. But I should temper my hope and my endeavors with the realities of the prison environment. With these realities in mind he said, I should continue to move in a positive direction and not be overly discouraged with what might happen as a result.

I remember hearing this, understanding it and even appreciating the words. But I also remember not liking what I heard. I recognized that I was in prison to be punished and that this carried with it certain mandates. But I also understood the logic of rehabilitation. If the public wanted the criminal to stop being criminal, then ways to encourage that to happen must be available. Yet, I was being told that, even given the desire, the ability and a substantially reasonable way to make that happen, chances were that it wouldn't and that I should simply come to grips with this fact.

This wasn't my first taste of the inconsistencies of the system, but it was the most real, the most personal. I realized at that very moment something a few others had told me but I had never actually felt for myself. That despite initiative, despite desire and despite capability, the system, even in the face of logic to the contrary, could hold one back. I also realized that one is put into a very uncomfortable position as this recognition sets in. You could accept the situation, the holding back by the system, as it is, as an unavoidable consequence of your environment. This would allow you to follow the advice of the chaplain, getting what you can with what is given. Or, you could attempt to re-shape the system, to change the environment, to alter the consequences. But, this is bucking the system, and this can be problematic, or, as the chaplain said, discouraging. Moreover, in a place like a prison, it could be very dangerous. Here, you had little control over yourself, let alone over the potentials for change. One could end up being an "enemy" of the administration, which could have an impact on when one gets released, or, as stories have it, even graver circumstances could result.

I thought about all this for the next several days. I really hadn't been prepared for this type of dilemma, which, in some senses, made me feel naive to circumstances commonplace to most of my fellow prisoners. And I also thought that perhaps I was making too big a deal out of what I should do. Perhaps all these concerns about changing the system or altering consequences were beyond the scope of me asking for an education program. Perhaps all I had to do was tell the prison administration that I had the abilities and the desire to develop an educational program, and that if they gave me the chance, I would make everyone look good. I decided to take this road, at least for the time being, at least until a real conflict developed. But, in making this decision, I realized that what I had felt in terms of accepting or challenging the system, the possible "catch 22" of it all, would not soon go away.

Sometimes when good fortune hits, it comes in bunches. Like when someone makes ten or twelve passes on the craps table, or wins four or five card hands in a row. So far, I had experienced a small run. I got out of county jail in a relatively short, three week's time. I was transported to the northern facility via private plane rather than bus. I had run into Sam who then told me about Joe. And I was now about to turn another lucky card. Still in the fish tank and several days after my meeting with the chaplain, I was scheduled to see the lead counselor at the prison, the person who interviewed all the new inmates regarding what each one might be thinking about, what their worries might be and what they wished to do or accomplish while incarcerated.

As I walked into the interview room I was astonished to see that the counselor had a familiar face. He was someone I had known from my earlier college days, someone I had, on occasion, actually partied with. We immediately shook hands and exchanged greetings. He said that he had already looked through my file, and thought that the inmate he was reading about was me, but that he was still surprised to see that it really was. He told me that after completing college he had obtained a counseling position in the prison system and that he was now on his way up the ladder. He then quickly moved the focus of our conversation to how I had ended up in prison and what I had in mind to do while there. I gave him a brief review of what I knew he already had in my file, and I also told him of my educational intent. He listened closely, and when I finished he responded much the same way the chaplain had.

There simply wasn't a program that could help me. He added that, given the bureaucratic process, even if the idea got off the ground, it might well be that I would be on the streets, on parole, before the program actually got implemented. But, he said, despite all the negatives, he did not mean that a program could not be started. He was the type who believed anything was possible, given the right time and the right place. Furthermore, he would do all that he could to help develop such a program if and when a proposal was made. And, if I needed any other assistance with anything else, his door would always be open to me.

So there I was, with a relatively important administrator who I could consider a friend. Someone who saw me as an old college mate who had taken a different path in life, as an individual who was now trying to turn things around. He wasn't someone who didn't trust me, who was chastising me for my behavior or who saw me primarily as a violent, drug-dealing deviant. As I returned to my cell I thought about how I now had an important person on my side, and how lucky I had been with this turn of events. I also had this notion that my luck was actually the residue of the educational program's design, that if I kept at the latter, the former would follow. I was convinced that I was on the right track.

Having completed all the tests and interviews, the final step before release onto the yard was a meeting with the classification committee. This group consisted of prison administrators: the warden, the program director, several counselors, the psychologist, the chaplain, the chief of the correctional officers (the captain), and educational and recreational staff. Their purpose was to review the information gathered during the fish tank stay assessing whether the inmate was fit for the general population. (i.e., was he stable enough?, was he enemy-free?), what program the inmate should be involved with (ie., drug or alcohol counseling, educational or vocational classes, etc.) and what type of job the inmate could or should do, if any jobs were indeed available. In terms of my case, they had before them someone who had been significantly involved in the narcotics trade, and this comma as has been mentioned, brings with it certain assumptions as to one's character. But I had no past felony convictions and no prior prison time served that might lend support to those assumptions. My psychological evaluations showed that I presented no mental problems and I had scored very well in the educational tests. And I was actually sitting in front of the committee--three of whose members, the psychologist, the chaplain and my friend, the counselor, I had already talked with--proposing, with great enthusiasm, that I be able to participate in a four-year college program.

As before, I was told that no such educational program existed. Moreover, the committee felt that they would need some type of assessment period to ascertain how I responded to yard life. I was not really in need of any counseling assistance, and because jobs were scarce I would have to take what was available. I was told that I would be released onto the yard in three days and that I would be assigned to work in the laundry. As I left the committee meeting room I wondered why they needed such an extensive process to come to these conclusions.

Upon release from the fish tank, I was sent to a unit that had a control center in its middle with three wings of dorm rooms and cells extending from that center. I was placed in the wing predominantly made up of white inmates (the other two were black, and Hispanic) in one of the dorm rooms, with about 12 other inmates. Each inmate had a bunk and a foot locker and at the end of the room were two showers and toilet facilities. It resembled a military barracks. I did not like the dorm room arrangement. Everything was too open and there were too many inmates with access to each other. I didn't care for the design of the entire unit actually, but this was, after all, the joint...and it was going to be my home for awhile.

I had my first meal on the yard that evening. I went down to the chow hall and got in the line that extended out the door. I had a constant eye out for my old pal Jughead but he was not in sight. One of my most memorable chow hall experiences occurred on that night. As the inmates passed through the first door to the chow hall, we were held back by a second door that was electronically controlled. This entrance door was opened as inmates exited through another parallel door, allowing the prison staff to control the room's numbers. As I entered that first door and waited for the second to open, I noticed another inmate on the exiting side slumped down against the wall, with blood soaked into his shirt. As is the rule, no inmates, coming or going, showed an interest in the situation. It wasn't until I got through the second door and had actually gotten my food that a guard became aware of the situation and some action to attend to the inmate began.

I knew the rules, and I had followed them just like everyone else. I was not very hungry at that moment, not happy with myself or the place, but I had little time to worry about it as I looked for a place to sit that wouldn't put me in the wrong company. As I said before, this was going to be my home for awhile!

The laundry turned out to be quite a place. It was a fairly large operation in the sense that it handled not only the prison clothing, i.e., jeans, shirts, underwear, socks, towels and sheets, but also the bed linen and towels from the local hospital and mental facility. There was, therefore, always a sufficient amount of work to be done. It would have turned out to be a very tedious situation, except that my old neighborhood pal and Vegas affiliate, Jughead, was already working there. I had been unable to locate him my first day on the yard, but now, unexpectedly, we were working side by side.

After a handshake and a hug, Jughead and I began to talk about old times, joking as we worked. We continued to do this on a daily basis, at times, laughing to the point of exhaustion, envisioning ourselves, two big shots from New York, doing what we were doing, drying and folding sheets. If only the boys could see us now!

But the laundry presented more than the opportunity to work and have fun with Jughead. It was there where several other inmates, inmates considered important on the yard, worked. And so the laundry provided the atmosphere in which to get to know these people.

The one man who was the best to get to know was a fellow named Hazen. He operated the pressing machine which steam pressed and then folded the prison-issued, jean shirts. He wasn't a particularly tall man, about 5'11", but he had a large and very strong frame, weighing about 240 pounds. His body was well covered with tattoos that promoted varying degrees of love and hate. And although the prison was filled with all sorts of tough guys, he had the reputation of being the "baddest."

Hazen was a member of the Hell's Angels and he was doing time for "an ex-felon in possession of a firearm" conviction. This conviction might not have been followed by a prison sentence, but he had only been out of prison for six months after serving 13 years in California's San Quentin Prison for murder. Therefore, authorities were quick to put him back behind bars. Hazen lived up to his Quentin reputation as he wouldn't hesitate to hurt and rumor had it, kill other inmates who crossed him, already battering a few while in Nevada. In future days, I would see him turn a very large, very intimidating inmate into an errand boy as a settlement to a confrontation which that inmate could no longer endure. But, in addition to being mean and violent, he could also think, imparting a wisdom that seemed to contradict his own life. He also had a sense of honor, a commitment to the ideas of fairness and justice and doing what was right. It was these elements, probably more than his badness, that gave him the respect that he clearly now had. I was fortunate in that Jughead had already established a friendship with Hazen. This made my introduction quite easy, and it wasn't long before he and I became the best of friends. And, I was indeed happy to have this friendship.

Our friendship began based on logical considerations. I had been touted by Jughead as an important man in the drug business, someone who was well connected and could make money. Jughead had also let it be known that I had taken the heat for the trouble with the police and that I had not given anybody over to them. This kind of information interested Hazen. He knew I was the trustworthy type, that I had some money and that I knew some important people. I would be a good guy to know.

I was certainly aware that having a friend with such a powerful presence was of value. As Hazen's pal, other inmates would think twice before attempting to cause me any discomfort. Additionally, through Hazen I was introduced to all the other heavyweights on the yard, individuals who had the reputation of being stand-up convicts. This almost immediately elevated my position within the prison hierarchy and made day-to-day life much more tolerable. So, like with most beginning friendships, Hazen and I recognized that we could be of benefit to each other.

But Hazen and I developed more out of this friendship. I began to talk with him about my plans for an education, about a future that had in it programs that helped ex-offenders both on an adult and juvenile level. I wanted his input, as someone who had experienced things differently from myself. And he gave it to me, often thinking about ideas for days before providing any comment. He wasn't cynical about any possibilities and he encouraged my thoughts, many times showing regret that he had simply wasted his own years. Hazen liked what we talked about, and he was seeing me as someone who might really do something different. We were still getting something from each other, perhaps boosting each other's character or providing positive energy between us, but we also developed a mutual respect for each other that would remain for the years that followed.

Life was tolerable during these times. I had been lucky (that word again) that Jughead was on the yard and that he knew Hazen and that I had made the acquaintances that I did. I now had a reputation as being one the boys, a member of the upper echelon of the prison world, and I was not bothered much by the struggles of the gangs and by those who had to fight every day to survive. This reputation was fueled even further by several inmates who, while awaiting their own sentencing on that day, had seen me sentenced in court in Las Vegas. As they now had arrived at the prison they told other inmates about me being a well-dressed and well-represented wise-guy, connecting that image to my current status on the yard. Bennie was also on the yard, and after he and I would exchange greetings, he would tell his Hispanic friends that I was the big shot who somehow managed to arrange our plane ride north.

So, amid the violence, the trouble and the noise, and aside from the bad food, bad doctoring and bad attitudes, and despite some poor administrative decisions and bureaucratic malfunctions, we managed to get along. We had our laughs at work, we had TV and a few movies to watch and we had recreational activities. We had prison sporting events to attend—we even tried to fix a boxing match but our guy got so weary from the lead in his gloves that he couldn't throw a straight punch—and we managed to cook a pasta dinner occasionally in one of the dorm rooms. But doing the time was also agonizingly boring and dull...perhaps the way it should be. Yet, I kept wondering what was being accomplished by all this. It seemed absurd to think that what we were doing would somehow have an impact on future criminality, that this would make criminals better or that the public would be safer. I couldn't understand it, but maybe I simply didn't know what some others did.

I also had visits from my old girlfriend, who was now, along with her brother, on the straight and narrow. But seeing her was equal parts of happiness and depression. She was like a fresh flower, bright and pretty, with a sweet and delicate fragrance. We would talk and kiss and steal some pleasures under the watchful eye of the guards in the visiting room. It was the best of the time. But when she had to leave, not to be seen for another month, the depression set in--the sensation of freedom and the deprivation of it clashing with each other.

Within the context of this life I was trying to balance my yard reputation and my continuing plea for an education program. Being one of the boys carried with it a certain set of responsibilities. These responsibilities centered on being a right guy. This meant that one would not walk away from confrontation, nor "let out" any information on what others might be doing. It also meant, at times, knowing about and even participating in behavior that could lead to serious problems.

With these kinds of responsibilities one is forced to stay keenly aware of the surrounding circumstances, to stay on top of his game in order that the right guy reputation stay intact. It's a difficult and wearing activity, and you have little room to escape its pressures. And I could not forget that I had an additional sentence hanging over my head should I get into trouble. Despite my outward coolness and my being in with the right crowd, I recognized that I was in a precarious situation. I hoped, and sometimes prayed, that I could manage to keep everything going as smoothly as it had.

While attempting to settle myself within the prison population, I also maintained my interest in developing an education program. I talked constantly with the administration, my counselor friend, and even the officers about any and all possibilities, and I followed up on every suggestion that was made. I was hoping that if I continued to keep the idea in the minds of those who could help, something might happen.

But I was also aware that my chances of getting a program were quite slim. I realized that the officials were watching the ease with which I handled the transition to yard life. They knew the crowd I was associated with and I recognized that this could make them a bit suspect of my academic intent. I had to consider that my time might be spent without an education program. So I continued living like one of the boys, a right guy, realizing that I would be better off getting through my time in this fashion if the program didn't develop. I didn't give up on the idea and tried as hard as I could to push the administration for some attention to the program's development, but I wasn't sure what was going to happen next.

Several months into my time I was told by the chief of the correctional officers, the captain, a man who I talked to about my educational ideas and who seemed genuinely interested in them, that a new prison was being opened in southern Nevada. He had visited the facility, seen its "new generation" design, and understood that it was to be a progressively-run institution. He also told me that inmates would be selected for transfer to that institution, and that although he couldn't promise me anything, I would stand as good a chance as anyone to make that transfer. As quick as I could arrange it, I met with my counselor friend and he too had the same information. He assured me that he would do all that he could to get me a transfer, but he cautioned that even with a transfer, an education program of the type I was hoping for might not be possible. He did agree that if it were at all possible in the system, the new place is where it would happen.

I was excited over this news. I immediately set up appointments with every administrator I could get to in order to lobby for my transfer down south. I was trying to convince them, as I had convinced myself, that I had to get there, that this might be my only chance to make an education program happen. A few more months passed, but I hadn't heard much about the transfers except that a process was in motion. It was common news on the yard now and others were hoping to make the trip as well. On a very cold winter morning I got called down to the administrative center where I was told to report to the captain's office. I was hoping that I would get some news on the transfer possibility, but his conversation threw me off. He asked me how I was doing, if things were going alright, if I had any problems, if I was still interested in education and if a transfer was still something I wanted. I was a bit angered by the situation but I responded with good, Okay, not really, yes, of course, all while wondering why I was in his office. He then let me have the news. He and my counselor friend had both recommended me for the transfer to the Southern Nevada Correctional Facility at Jean, Nevada, and I had been selected to go. I would be leaving, along with about 40 others, in less than a month's time.

I shook the captain's hand with as much thankfulness as I could display and asked if I could see my counselor friend. I was told he had left for a vacation but that he knew about the transfer, and that he was happy for me. As I left the administrative center and walked across the yard, everything seemed to whirl around in my mind.

The jail, the plane, Bennie, Sam, Jughead, Hazen, my college-mate counselor, the captain, my family...What if things hadn't gone the way they did? What if I hadn't gotten the transfer? What would I be thinking about if that occurred? I had been very lucky so far, blessed as best as I could fathom. I wasn't assured of getting my education program together, or of finding that kind of redemption from my past, but I had made a big step in that direction. I could feel the energy which seemed to spring from my education plan. I was convinced it had me on the right path.

Jughead and Hazen were happy to hear about the transfer, and they were hoping to make it to the new facility in the near future as well. By then, they joked, I should have the place in order. It wasn't long before the paperwork for the transfer was completed, and I was ready to leave. We said our good-byes with emotion, the way any people do who share a common experience. It was early morning when, handcuffed and in leg irons, I boarded the bus with 40 other inmates headed for the new prison in Jean, just 30 miles west of Las Vegas.

Chapter 3

THE NEW PLACE

I was chained at mid-waist to two other inmates prior to being led to the bus. As I boarded, shuffling along with my fellow travelers, I laughed to myself about how different this was from my original trip north...suit, plane and all. Nonetheless, I was happy to be going, one way or the other. The day was rainy and the bus ride was uncomfortable and long. My chain-mates were two guys I would eventually come to know and like. J.T. was a black man, tall and well built, in his late thirties. He had bushy, long hair, graying a bit, and a gold tooth with his initials inscribed on it. He was very quiet during the trip but I found out later that he had done time throughout his life for drugs, pimping and burglary. He evidently had a promising baseball career, making it to the minors, until the drug life got the better of him. (J.T. would later become a member of a softball team I put together which would win the prison championship. The game was won over the protest of the other team's captain, as he noticed that I slipped J.T. into the line-up twice in the last inning, giving J.T. the chance to hit the game winning triple.)

My other mate was a short, stocky, Hispanic man, with wavy black hair and a thick mustache. His name was George and he, too, had been in and out of prison most of his life, mostly for heroin-related offenses. It seemed that he would, when incarcerated, find God as his source of inspiration, encouraging prison officials to tender him release. But, once on the streets, George would inevitably find the "power of the poppy" better suited for his inspiration and his troubles would start all over again. (George, too, would become a member of our softball team. He possessed an underhand knuckle ball that was almost impossible to hit out of the infield.)

Our trip was uneventful and not much was said between us, though we did have to rely on each other when one of us decided to smoke. Being handcuffed it was easier for the fellow sitting next to you to reach in your front shirt pocket for a cigarette and light. This provided several occasions where a few words were exchanged, but only a few. We made a stop in mid-state Nevada, at an old hotel in an old, once-popular, mining town. We were provided with a bag lunch from the hotel, which we had to eat outside in the parking lot, and the opportunity to use the bathroom facilities. This caused quite a scene as we milled around in our prison issues, in leg-irons and well guarded, while the townspeople stared at us like they might at unsightly livestock. I wasn't sure whether I wanted to cower or to growl, but as we were herded back into the bus, the thought of both passed.

When we arrived in Jean some 14 hours later we could feel the warm weather of southern Nevada. It was early evening and the desert sky was magnificently clear, lightening everyone's travel-weary thoughts. We could see the facility from a distance, lit up like a birthday cake. As we pulled into the main gate, we could easily tell that it was a prison, but one with new everything—new buildings, new wire fences, even the guards seemed new.

We were unloaded and escorted to a unit that was situated in the middle of about six others. All the units were designed around a shrub-filled, grassy lawn that enclosed a large running track with a football-sized field at its center. It was not a large facility, having a gym on one end, an administrative center on the other, and a school and library in between. On a little hill overlooking the units was the chow hall, a small commissary, a barber shop and a medical center. Everything was in sight of everything else, making the work for the guards in the two towers placed on opposite ends of the facility as easy as it could be.

We were led to a building that was the equivalent of the fish tank of the northern facility, except it was all new and it had much better accommodations. There was a control office where the guards looked out on a central meeting area that was covered by a thick rug. New, cushioned chairs were scattered about this space and a large TV was at the center. There were two tiers of cells that ran three quarters of the way around the central area and heavy metal doors on each cell. We were led to the cells, one for each of us, and told to wait for further instructions. As each of us gazed into our new living quarters, with a new bed, stainless steel toilet and sink, desk and chair, and small storage cabinet, we realized, at least from this line of sight, that this was indeed a different kind of place.

We waited a few minutes and we were then reconvened in the central area, as the warden and several of his assistants were introduced to us. It was late and everyone was tired, but our inmate group was brought alive by this introduction. Accompanying the warden and his co-workers were several guards, two of whom were female. As I looked at the faces of my fellow travelers I could see that the warden was going to have to work to gather our full attention.

The warden ran through the ideas behind the new facility. It was built with state-of-the-art design and management in mind, allowing inmates to be treated with respect and fairness in an environment that suggested both. There would be jobs for most inmates, as well as school and counseling programs and plenty of recreational opportunities available. The correctional staff, which was about one-third female, had been encouraged through their training to be helpful to the inmates and sensitive to the problems that could occur in a prison environment.

This was a small facility where it was anticipated that the inmates would get enough attention so that a change toward civilized behavior could take place. The warden emphasized that, given all the amenities, it would be expected that we would get involved in the programs available to us and that we would do so while showing to all others, inmates and staff alike, the same respect and fairness shown to us. In fact, he said, we had been selected to come to Jean because it was felt we had that kind of potential.

If this could happen, we, as well as other inmates who passed through the facility, might be better able to find our way out of returning to prison. Furthermore, the staff would find themselves in jobs that they didn't mind coming to every day. This new SNCC facility would, in other words, come to represent a successful rehabilitative model, and we were being relied upon to help get the place up and running. The warden closed by letting us know that our specific questions would be attended to the following day, as would an explanation of our daily activities, job possibilities and other administrative matters.

Our general introduction was complete and we were led to our quarters with the metal doors secured behind us. I wasn't clear on all the models that existed as alternatives to this one, but I liked what the warden said, and I liked the way this place looked and felt. As I slipped into my new bed, new sheets and all, I thought about how fortunate I was to be there, and how well my plan for an education fit with what the warden had talked about. I said my now nightly prayer of thanks, hoping as well for the blessings to continue.

I was astonished when at 6 a.m. the following morning a guard came to my door, unlocked it and said, "Good morning, it's wake-up time." This was quite a departure from the jail and northern facility and I had to admit that it made me feel a bit strange, almost as if I wasn't really in prison. But I was relieved that the previous day's activities weren't some type of twisted dream, and I dressed quickly, anxious for the day to develop.

After breakfast was delivered to us in the unit, we were assembled in the center of the unit for another meeting. This time, there were several administrators who were going to provide us with an explanation of our duties and responsibilities, what we could expect our day-to-day activities to be like and what jobs and programs were available. After a review of the rules and regulations, we were told that the daily routine would be much like that of any other institution. This meant that we would be up at 6 a.m., except for those assigned to an early detail, with an "off the yard and into your unit" curfew of 9 p.m. Lights out would be at 11 p.m., with everyone expected to be in their room at that time. A count would be taken four times a day--a process where inmates are to be in their rooms or at a designated work station allowing the administration to count all the inmates in order that everyone be accounted for--and mealtimes would run for an hour and a half, 6:30 to 8 a.m. for breakfast, 12 to 1:30 p.m. for lunch and 4:30 to 6 p.m. for dinner. During work hours, generally from 8:30 to 4:30 p.m. excluding lunch, all inmates were expected to be at their posts unless they had a signed pass to be at the medical or administrative center or they were participating in one of the available counseling or educational programs.

The gym would be open throughout the day with team events and recreational programs developed through the recreational director's office. It was anticipated that the prison would organize teams in several sports that would compete against others brought in from outside agencies, like the police, sheriff's department or university. We could also expect, as part of recreation, that films and even live entertainment shows would occasionally be brought in. This, of course, would be predicated on our behavior prior to, during and after any events.

General visitation days would be Thursday through Sunday, 9 a.m. to 5 p.m. each day. When visitors did come, they would sign in to be cleared by the staff. In the meantime, inmates would be notified of the visit and called down to the visiting room area accordingly. An inmate could then expect to be searched both coming into the visit, usually a "pat-down" check, and going from it, usually a strip search complete with an anal "gaze." One could also expect a visit to be denied or allowed only via phone and through glass if a visitor was deemed to pose a problem. There were no conjugal visits.

We were told that everyone would be assigned a job, but that any inmate could apply for a specific job if he had certain skills that matched with the position. Some of the these type positions involved masonry or carpentry skills, or office or medical skills and these type jobs would usually pay more on the inmate wage scale. As for pay, every job would be rated as to its technical difficulty and the pay would range accordingly. All of the jobs paid very little, but what one did make would be placed on his inmate account. This account, which could also include other money that the inmate had, could be used to buy toiletries, small food items (chips, cookies, soda, etc.) or cigarettes at the prison commissary. Via an inmate I.D., which was to be issued the following day, one could charge the purchase of goods to their account number listed on their I.D. At the end of one's time, any money that was accumulated from this account, as well as the state-issued two hundred dollar hit-the-road sum, would be given to the inmate.

With this general information out of the way, we were asked if we had any questions. I immediately raised my hand to ask about the potential of any college programs being initiated at the facility, as I hadn't heard any mention of this possibility. One of the administrators responded that nothing like this had been developed, but that in the future, this might be something that the administration might consider. I was worried with hearing this future-based response, even though it was positive in its nature. I knew enough about the system. It tended to move very slow on new ideas, if it moved at all. But, I couldn't focus very long on this worry. We had each been assigned a counselor who we were now going to get to meet. We were told that if we had any ideas about job assignments or anything else, this would be the person to talk with. I had my eye on a particular job, and I also wanted to continue to push for an education program possibility, so I prepared myself to talk with my counselor.

The sequence of events that followed served to strengthen my belief that the power of a God, and that of luck, were on my side. My counselor's name was Terry, a tall, rangy-built, German-Irish looking man, only a few years older than myself. He had longish red-brown hair, a Fumanchu styled mustache and a very intense-looking face. He seemed like a nice chap as he offered me a chair and asked if I would like some coffee. He told me that I was the fourth man he was seeing that day and he still had five more to go, so he needed his coffee.

When he asked what he could do for me, I immediately went into discussing my hope for an education program. I told him about my background and how I was planning on using education as the means for turning my life around, and how the idea had so far gotten me to Jean. I could see as I talked that he was interested in what I was saying.

When I was finished, he quickly asked me what area of study I would want to focus on. He was the first person who actually posed that type of question and I was encouraged as it seemed to move the possibility of getting an education up a notch. I wasn't sure what exactly I wanted to get into, but I told him that I was interested in politics and that I had taken a few of those courses when I attended school in upstate New York. It turned out that he, too, was interested in politics, and that he had spent a great deal of his undergraduate and graduate work with that subject. We proceeded to talk for almost an hour, well beyond the allotted 20 minutes per inmate, as we bantered back and forth about politics and economics and the relationship of one to the other.

We seemed to be hitting it off and he had me thinking about many of the points he had made. But as he noticed the time, he had to quickly change our focus to what I had in mind in terms of working in the institution. I told him that I would like to apply for the position of work-release clerk, a job that would entail typing, filing and being an assistant to the work release program director. I told him that I realized that I would have a typewriter and paper and other office supplies at my access, and that this would help should I get an educational program off the ground. I also noted that I liked the rank of the job, as it was situated at the top of the pay scale.

When I finished I noticed a wry smile on Terry's face, an expression I would come to understand to mean that something's up. He told me that, aside from being a unit counselor, in charge of the inmates housed in one of the five new units, he was also the director of the work-release program. He would be the one responsible for hiring the person for the (his) clerk's position. He had several other people who had inquired about the job and he expected that others would be forthcoming. But, while shaking my hand and noting the time, he said that he had enjoyed our chat and that he would make a decision on the job the following day. I should stop by and see him then, as he also wanted to speak a bit more about the education plan.

I left his office feeling confident about the impression I had made, and I knew I had a good chance of getting the job. It was another stroke of luck that I got assigned to the counselor who just happened to be the director of the program I wanted to work at. There were four other counselors I could have gotten connected to, but I got him...and he seemed like a nice guy to boot.

I felt good and I spent the rest of the day getting acquainted with the yard. We were allowed to go outside of our unit, to see what the place actually looked like, and so I took advantage of that possibility.

I went to the gym, the library, the medical center, and the chow hall. I met up with J.T. and George and we had our lunch as we talked about the newness of everything...the lawns, the shrubs, the brick, the steel, the basketballs, the pool tables, the windows, the carpets, the televisions, the beds, the tables, the chairs, even the dishes and forks. We were all lucky to be a part of this newness and it was clear that we three recognized this, as we shared a smoke, smiled a bit and walked the yard.

I was up before the 6 a.m., good morning wake-up. I felt a sense of immediacy to the day. Once my door was unlocked, I showered and then went with J.T. and George for breakfast. Our early morning chat centered around the female guards, and how a few of them looked like they could be in Playboy. There was no doubt that each of us was conjuring up images of exactly what that might look like as we left the chow hall and proceeded back to the unit.

At about 10 a.m., I was summoned to Terry's office. He greeted me with a handshake and a congratulations as he told me that I had been selected to fill the position of work-release clerk. I began to thank him for his choice but he waived me off saying that he thought he had more important news. He told me that he had talked with the prison psychologist the previous night about our conversation regarding an education program. She was an old college chum of his, and she was also married to a professor in the criminal justice department at the University of Nevada at Las Vegas. It seemed that she and Terry considered that it might be through him that a program could be developed. Terry asked me if I wanted to talk with her about this, especially in light of the fact that I, like all the other inmates, would have to eventually talk with the psychologist anyway.

I was in a brief stupor. I had gotten the job I wanted and now this man I had just met the day before was talking to me about actually developing an education program. I tried to keep my usual cool demeanor, but I was excited. I told Terry I would be ready as soon as a meeting could be arranged. I could see that Terry was happy as well. He could feel perhaps that he was getting a chance to do the work that counselors so often can't do. He told me that he would type out a pass for me to see the psych that afternoon, and that I should tell her exactly what I had told him.

As I shook hands with him again, expressing as sincere a thank you as I could manage, he told me he had one other item to take care of. He then handed me a book and told me to begin reading it as soon as I could. As I walked out the door, looking at the cover of Richard Quinney's *Critique of Legal Order*, Terry said with that wry smile, "You may end up not liking me for giving you that book!"

After lunch I was handed a pass by one of the guards in our unit that cleared me to see the psychologist. I proceeded to the administration center where her office was located. She was expecting me. She was about 30 and I immediately noticed her tight-fitting sweater and incredible-looking figure. As we sat to talk I also noticed that her face reflected a sort of confusion which made me think she was a bit unsure of herself. I told her much of the same things I told Terry and she listened without speaking a word. Her quietness made me nervous, but when I finished she told me that she thought my ideas had merit and that she was in total agreement that educational programs were indeed something that the institution should develop. Given the tight sweater and that confused look, it was difficult to concentrate on her conversation. But I realized that I had an ally in her, and that her endorsement of my ideas, especially as the prison psych, would be important.

Just as I thought that our discussion had ended, she asked me if I would like to meet her husband, the professor in the criminal justice department at UNLV. It seemed that he was in the prison vault collecting statistics for a book he was writing and that I could meet with him that afternoon. I wasn't at all prepared for such an immediate opportunity, and I had to pinch myself to believe I was hearing what I just heard. As I walked to the vault I was again feeling that surge of luck that seemed to be a part of everything that was happening.

When I got to the vault, Randy was waiting for me. He was about six feet tall with a medium build, scholarly-looking with horned-rimmed glasses and a tweed coat. He seemed like a nice guy as he extended his hand with a "pleased to meet you" right behind it. I could sense that we were both a bit nervous, me for meeting a professor, and him for actually chatting with an inmate similar to those he had written about.

I told him about my desire to get an education while incarcerated and how fortunate I had been up to the point of our meeting. I also told him that I wasn't sure of what I wanted to study, but that I had talked with Terry about a political science possibility. He then told me about his criminal justice program, and his own interest in what was happening with the prison systems in America. He liked the idea of helping to put together an inmate education program, although he wasn't sure how it could happen. He remarked that independent studies, perhaps two, might be a good way for us to get started. I responded, sensing the "us" and the possibility that something was actually going to happen, that anything he could think of would be fine by me.

Randy asked if I was interested in getting a cup of coffee, and he suggested that we walk over to the chow hall for some fresh air to get it. I was more than happy to oblige him and as we walked and talked I sensed several more things. Randy seemed almost as excited as I was. He was making friends with a real inmate, someone he could actually talk with. He would be able to obtain some valuable information for his book through me, and also help me at the same time. Like with Terry, he was getting the chance to do something people in his profession didn't usually get.

I was enjoying our conversation as we walked, especially recognizing that Randy could be the conduit through which my education plan developed. As we finished our coffee, we shook hands with mutual respect. He told me that he would look into what he needed to do in order for some type of program to be initiated, and that he would be in touch with me within a week's time. I walked back to my unit in a fog of positive thought.

When I got back to the unit I told Terry all that had happened and he, too, was excited. He told me that he would again talk with the psych and her husband to ascertain their perceptions about what should happen next. He suspected that if an independent study process was suggested, we would have to get acceptance from the SNCC classification committee for it to happen. This, he said, would take a bit of politicking, and he thought that I should make an appointment with the warden as soon as possible in order that he know what was developing. Terry said that he would help arrange the meeting which would then move the idea into a more formal setting. He then told me that I was dismissed for the day, that I had had enough for one day anyway and that I should go and read my new book. I could officially start my new job the next day.

I laid on my bunk, thinking about what was going on. Things were happening as I had hoped and prayed, to the extent that they didn't even seem real. I tried to calm myself over my anxious thoughts, thinking of the old convict adage "hope for the best but expect the worst." But I had already gotten too much from my hopes for that to really stick. I picked up the book Terry had given me, deciding that the reading would put my focus elsewhere. Little did I realize that, on top of everything else that was swirling around me, I would settle into a book that would have a profound impact on the rest of my life.

I had no idea what to expect from *The Critique of Legal Order*. Aside from his caveat, Terry hadn't said anything about it, and I wasn't sure of its contents even after reading the reviews on the book's cover. So it was with a sense of complete astonishment that I read through what Quinney was saying. He was making a case for the skewed nature of our legal system. At the core of his case was something I had felt and actually witnessed in my life, that the process of making money had its downside. I already knew that the pursuit of money had gotten me into trouble.

But it was Quinney's connection of this simple "money is the root of all evil" notion to the mechanics of capitalism that hit me as a form of revelation. For those who can remember, I recall the sensation as being similar to the light bulb going on in the old Ford Motor commercial.

According to Quinney, we live in a capitalist system, as opposed to the democracy and free enterprise mix we are accustomed to hearing about. This system is controlled by the rich and powerful. More to the point, it is controlled by those who control production and profit. These people come to make laws primarily out of their own interests, with the idea of increasing or at least maintaining their profit and power. Concomitantly, our legal institutions come to reflect these same interests, which means that the law and our system of jurisprudence come to favor the rich and powerful. Subsequently, principles like fairness, justice and equality often get bent before the law, with two levels of justice actually developing, one for the rich and one for the others. And, unfortunately, the government, which also acts on behalf of the rich and powerful, is not of value in addressing this problem. Rather than being a mediator for "all the people," the government responds as an agent for those in power, which actually makes it part of the problem, not a true partner in the problem's solution.

I had never read, heard, nor thought of anything like this before. I was amazed that the type of behavior that I had witnessed in the streets and in the courtrooms could be so well described within the context of a capitalist system. The intricate analysis and the varied information that Quinney utilized in support of his assumptions were also amazing, although their detail is beyond our immediate scope. But the more I read, the more sense his observations made. Everything seemed so very consistent with the realities of the American process.

So there I was, not sure of all that I was reading, but recognizing with thunderous clarity that what I was reading had more relevancy to things than anything else I had ever read. I finished a good portion of the short book before I fell asleep and I awoke early and read more. When my door was unlocked I was ready for my new job, ready to talk with the warden about my educational program, ready to read more, ready to talk with Terry about the reading... "ready to go" in prison. And I had only been in Jean for four days!

Chapter 4

GETTING OUT

[Lest the reader think otherwise, I need to interject a few thoughts, now being as good a time as any. The rest of this chapter will continue to chart the course for the development of my educational process and the analytical perspective that followed. There will be some mention of circumstances or situations that occurred in conjunction with these points, but, for the most part, the day-to-day activities of prison life are not documented. This means that the tediousness of the routine, the abject loneliness and bouts with despair will not be highlighted. This means that the viciousness, vulgarity, and even the touches of kindness, will go mostly without reference. This means that the card games, pool games, ball games and people games won't be emphasized. This means that the drug running (you name it, we had it), the booze making (a migraine-guaranteeing, banshee-producing, tastes-like-piss-smells, fruit and sugar concoction called pruno) and the tattoo fashioning (some of the most "thoughtful" designs in the world) won't be talked about. This means that the characters like Vito, "the hitter" (a strong-man for the mob), Fat Jack (a person who, having done time all over the world, made himself quite comfortable in the prison environment), One-Armed Pete (an armed robber who took delight in that symbolism), Mayonnaise (a young man so named because his brain was affected by heroin cut with dried battery acid), Mama Greene (the "madam" of the facility) and all the others, will, for the most part, go unexplored. I regret all these omissions, but with the task at hand, it must be this way.

But, do not forget that these kinds of occurrences and these kind of people permeate prison life. And, as they comprise the places and faces that were part of my experiences, they are as important to the fabric of my understanding as any books I will ever encounter. With that being said...and hopefully remembered...we will move on.]

If one could hand pick a warden amenable to an education program, Ed P. would be the choice. In fact, he had been hired by the state to manage the new rehabilitative-style facility because he was very much in favor of that philosophy. My ideas were right on target with what he was already thinking. He listened intently to my plan, and I could tell he was noting both my sincerity and desire. I would take two independent studies from Randy to prove that my abilities matched my desire. This would mean that Randy would bring in the reading material, and I would be responsible for completing written assignments associated with that material. If I were successful with this process, I would then appeal to the prison administration for additional classes, maybe even for the privilege of attending school.

Ed P. liked the idea, saying that this was the type of progressive program he was hoping to bring to the Nevada prison system. However, he did make it clear that the decision for such an undertaking was one he could not make alone. The plan would have to be passed by the SNCC classification committee to be implemented. I told him that Terry and I had already discussed this, and that we were prepared to do whatever was necessary to advance the plan. The warden said that he would schedule the idea for consideration at the following month's committee meeting, and that what happened there would dictate what would come next.

As I left his office, I was again excited about the prospects. The warden seemed to be another ally, and this would carry a great deal of weight come meeting time. I also had the psych on my side and, of course, Terry, and both were on the committee. I figured that I would also lobby the captain, the chaplain, the program director, and the person in charge of the secondary education programs, explaining to them exactly what I had explained to the warden. It was clear that if I could garner their support as individuals, I would be assured of the committee's approval. I didn't realize it at the time, but in addition to doing what I needed to do to forward my education plan, I was also learning a skill that would help me with future endeavors.

I did have difficulty persuading the captain, the man in charge of the correctional officer (guard) staff, about the plan, as well as the program director. The captain felt that a program of this nature would eventually be problematic because he would have to arrange special duties for his correctional officers designed around the program. This meant that someone would have to check the books being sent or brought in for me, and if I were eventually given the chance to actually attend school, guards would have to be spared for my transport and care. He did not like that one inmate would get such special attention, and he feared that if the program was extended to other inmates, then it would become even be more of a problem. Additionally, and this was probably his main objection, his philosophy of incarceration was based on the idea that inmates should go to prison to be punished. Although he knew the SNCC tone was at odds with this philosophy, he seemed like one of those people who felt an obligation to uphold the old school principles. I didn't realize it at the time, but this "what to do with inmates" debate represented the major dividing line between liberal and conservative politics, particularly as it related to how money and resources were to be used in the correctional system. For fear of getting ahead of myself, I will return to these points a bit later.

The program director's objections seemed directed more at my person than at any philosophical concerns. He had this notion that I was simply a slick, New York-type who was finding a way to "get over" on the system. To him, I was someone who had been an operator on the streets, and I was now attempting to create that same type situation in the joint. In simple words, the man neither liked nor trusted me.

I wasn't at all happy with these two positions, although I certainly respected the captain's objection's over those of the program director's. Both bothered me in that I perceived the education program as something that would make everyone look good, and I also saw myself as someone who could be relied upon to do what he was promising to do. But neither man seemed impressed with my thoughts. I decided to chalk this up to experience. I remember hoping that objections of this kind would always remain with the minority of those who mattered.

The next month I spent working at my job and politicking for my program. As to the latter, Randy had already done his part in organizing several courses that I could take and he had gotten the approval of the university to allow the process to develop. This was an enormous step and it helped me to sell the program. And, as to the former, not only was my work with Terry very interesting, but it coincided perfectly with my education plan and lobbying efforts.

The work-release program was a process whereby inmates, within two months of their release date, could go out to work each day, returning to the prison at night. This would allow the inmate the chance to earn money, some of which would go to pay for his prison lodging, while also re-acclimating him to the outside world. In general, the program provided a test for both the inmate and the prison officials as to whether the inmate was actually ready for release.

As the work-release clerk, I served as Terry's assistant, helping to develop and then implement the new project. I was therefore involved with the ground floor work, developing job opportunities, placing inmates in those jobs, organizing time schedules for departures and arrivals and maintaining records for pay deposits and inmate food, lodging and transportation costs. Importantly, my job kept me in continual contact with the administration as Terry and I worked out the details of the program. With every opportunity that this contact presented (and recognizing the possibilities, Terry made sure I had many of them), I would note my education plan, chatting with the administrators who would soon vote on its potential. I was in an ideal position, working with a great boss at an interesting job that happened to provide me access to the right people.

In the midst of our work, Terry and I organized a proposal for the classification committee meeting, outlining what I had been talking about for the last several months as well as what Randy had been able to arrange at the university. I submitted this to the committee as I addressed them with my idea. It wasn't a difficult process, as I had already talked with almost all the members beforehand. Within a day, and over the two objections that I suspected were forthcoming, the committee passed my independent study request. For the upcoming term, I was going to be allowed to take two courses, one in criminal justice, the other in political science. I was ecstatic. Through all the twists and turns, it had actually happened. I realized that I was on my way now, with an education program in my grasp and a providential hand squarely on my shoulder.

I had been corresponding with my family on a regular basis, and as it had been from the beginning, their support was a constant buoy. Through their letters and my once-a-week, collect phone calls I was not only able to feel their love but also to reinforce my energy for what I was doing. So what happened next, only days after the committee approval, served to rock my world unlike anything else had ever done.

I received a message in my unit that I was to report to the administrative center because of an emergency phone call. I had no idea what this could be about, but I knew it wasn't good. At the center I was told to call my sister in New York because she had called earlier requesting to talk with me about a serious family situation. I was afraid to call, and as I heard her voice on the line I realized that my fears were justified.

My mother had suffered an aneurysm, a dilating blood clot that had lodged itself in her neck, in such a delicate position that it could not be surgically attended to. The situation was grim. It was likely that the clot would explode, either killing my mother or leaving her paralyzed. There was a one-in-twenty chance that it could dissolve itself. This was apparently what the doctors and my family had agreed was really the only livable option. Even at that, the effect this trauma would have on her could not be perceived. She lay in a coma at the hospital, as last rites were being discussed. When I asked my sister what had caused the injury to happen, I sunk in all spirit, body and mind. She told me that it was caused by an overload of stress. Although she never inferred it, I knew immediately that the real cause of my mother's problem was me.

I crawled back to my unit and proceeded directly to my bunk. I lay there, numb and shaky, envisioning my mother and all the good things that embodied her motherhood. I wept. What a despicable creature I was—a drug dealer, a gangster. My mother's son in prison while she lay agonizing, dying from wounds I inflicted. What image did she have of me at this moment? Would she die with the image of her "convict son" on her mind...in her heart? My tears seemed as much for me as for her, and this selfishness only made the tears come harder. I was at the lowest point in my life.

The day passed with nothing else on my mind. I talked to Terry about the situation and he was very kind. And, after they noticed my sullen mood, I told a few of my inmate friends. Between inmates there isn't much room for emotion of this kind, particularly on the giving end. But what little there was came my way. I was able to phone my father, and, as might be suspected, he was beside himself over what had happened. He talked to me about what he would do should my mother, his wife of 30-plus years, pass on. Yet he, like my sister, never alluded to the idea that what had transpired developed from my doing. Instead, he encouraged me to stay steady on my educational course. He stressed that no matter what happened, he, like my mother, wished only the best for me. Despite the despair, my father gave me hope.

At Terry's suggestion I went to speak with the chaplain, Father Barry, about the possibility of obtaining a temporary release to see my mother one last time. Father Barry and I had become friends (we would remain so even after my release), and I trusted him to do what he could to secure such a release. After discussing the matter with the administration, he told me that a pre-death release was not an option. But, upon my mother's death, a release was possible and he would certainly help out should that occur.

I called my sister every day that week, talking about our mother's condition, about the family and about my education program. She was in as much agony as me, but she managed to talk with all her courage about these things, trying to ease my pain through her own. She was certainly another blessing. In fact, she and her husband would name their first boy, born while I was still in prison, after me!

After a week of worry, my sister told me that, miraculously, my mother's condition was improving. It seemed that the slimmest of possibilities had occurred, that due to her strong physical state, and a strong will, the aneurysm was dissolving itself. As this was occurring, she was regaining her motor skills and even beginning to recognize and speak to people. The doctors had indicated that as the dissolving process continued, my mother would be, with only a few short-term affects, as good as new.

My emotions were battered, and I returned to my day in a state of bewilderment. I was happy. My prayers had once again been answered. Luck was again on my side. But the fragility of both was apparent and I was afraid. In my self-absorbed existence, I had not really considered the question of mortality—surprisingly, not even my own. But now I felt it and I sensed that state of urgency that follows. I vowed again to work as hard as I could to make myself into something, to redeem myself in the eyes of those who mattered. My mind slipped back into the education program that was now actually going to happen. I was so very, very fortunate...I had a chance.

The first two independent studies provided me with a great many thoughts about America. In the political science course, I was given books that discussed many of the principles from which our country developed. The authors included the likes of Hobbes, Locke, Rousseau, Jefferson and Hamilton. I enjoyed reading the material, and the papers that I was assigned were mainly focused on how the ideas for our democracy developed as they did.

Many of the readings I received in my criminal justice course however, followed the logic that Richard Quinney had presented in his *Critique of the Legal Order.* Various authors like Tony Platt and David Gordon presented what was referred to as a "critical analysis of capitalism." It was this analysis, based on Karl Marx's observations about the nature of capitalism, that I found most provocative.

In a nutshell (and I recognize that I am taking many liberties here, leaving out details and supportive footnotes), the analysis described how, in a system that focused on profit development over human development, competition over cooperation and an exploitation of the majority of people (i.e., the workers), a class system would develop and certain inequalities would result. These inherent inequalities would then affect the actualization of principles like justice and fairness, and they would also translate into other social problems like poverty, unemployment, racism and sexism, all of which would impact the occurrence of crime. According to this logic, then, in a capitalist system, and the argument is that America is clearly of this order, attempts at successfully addressing social problems like crime would be fruitless unless the system itself, which actually creates and perpetuates these problems, is addressed and, ultimately, dismantled. In this process, the concepts of socialism and communism, concepts that promised primary focus on human and social concerns versus profit, could be developed.

I didn't necessarily want to believe all this, but, as with Quinney, I was impressed with what these authors were saying. It all seemed so consistent with what my experiences had shown me. Moreover, I was intrigued by the critical analysis logic as it compared to what we generally learn about America. I had always been taught that America was a democracy where participation in government was balanced and where things like justice, fairness and equality were restricted more by our own prejudices than anything else. I was taught that our political system, the government, served to broker all our interests, primarily for the benefit of the people. We had an economic system, usually referenced as free enterprise, which was seemingly distinct from our political system. This system of supply and demand, and private ownership, struggled to provide us all with work opportunities, goods and services. In fact, much of what I was reading in my political science course mirrored this image.

Yet, these teachings appeared at odds with what one actually saw happening in America, especially considering how significantly money and power influence and control our political process, our legal system, our educational arena and almost everything else one could think of. The Marxist perspective seemed to make more sense and this peaked my curiosity. And I began to question why, despite its closeness to our reality, I, or we, had never heard much about a critical Marxist analysis, except in relationship to Communist China, or the Soviet Union or Cuba—our enemies. Weren't we at least half like Marx proposed? Wasn't there some relevance to Marxist thought that would help us better understand America? Shouldn't we at least know about a philosophy that references our society, one that half the world, and maybe more, supports? Would not knowing about this analysis make us appear blind to the rest of the world? Shouldn't we be provided with an education, beginning in our secondary processes, that included such important information... information that might help us improve our nation?

Through my readings a logical answer to these questions became apparent. According to Marxists, the rich and powerful formed our ideology, and that was the reason we learned some things and not others. Therefore, an education of the sort that criticized the system for what it was (i.e., capitalist) and suggested alternatives to it (i.e., socialism and communism) might well pose a threat to that system and to those (the rich and powerful) who profit most from it. It would make sense then that, if we learned anything at all about Marxism, it would be framed in the context of an enemy's philosophy.

This possibility angered me. I didn't want to agree with its totality (I would continue to struggle with this "domination of ideology" idea), but I was pushed to consider that most of us were being duped in America, that people and processes were at work that fooled us into believing that we were something that we were not. I was, for the first time in my life, becoming politicized and I wrote several of my papers with these points in mind. I would present the logic of the radical/Marxist writers, along with my developing frustrations, and, although my interpretations needed work, what I submitted always impressed my professors.

I completed my first two independent studies and earned an A in each. More importantly, I was on fire over education. I wasn't sure whether what I was thinking, particularly the questioning of our American process, came as a result of the books that I was provided. Perhaps I was being persuaded to think a certain way. I also considered that perhaps my growing radicalism was a function of being in prison. As I read about concepts like exploitation and oppression—important concerns of the radical, Marxist analysis—it might have been that, given where I was, I could too readily identify with those effects. So I needed to know more.

Given my success with the first two courses, I decided to ask the classification committee for permission to enroll as a full-time student. I applied for and received a Pell Grant, which allowed me to pay for a full-time program, and which gave me a sort of federal recognition for what I was doing. I also had the total support of the university as the people there realized that something good was happening. With all this in hand, I approached the committee and asked to take 15 credits that term, as I was hoping to complete my degree before my first parole hearing. I also asked permission for a once-a-week release to make the one-hour trip to campus. This would allow me the chance to attend classes and talk with my professors. I stressed that I would continue to hold my job as the work-release clerk in addition to working at the proposed education program. Over the same two objections (the captain now joined the program director in seeing me as someone getting over on the system), I was given the opportunity for the full-time program. My request for a release process, which I realized was a bit presumptuous at that juncture, was summarily denied. Nonetheless, I was more than happy with the committee's decision, and I settled into a routine of school, work and prison life that would consume the next 20 months.

As I noted, my job was very interesting. My duties brought me in contact with a good number of inmates and staff alike. I got to see how a new program developed, what problems occurred and how both inmates and administrators responded to those problems. In essence, I got to see how close a program might come to reach its intended effects, and the reasons for its successes and failures.

The work-release process was conceptually sound. It offered inmates the chance to make some money, and got them out into the public, away from the joint every day. However, in a practical sense, most jobs were dead-end opportunities, the "hot and sweaty, Las Vegas laundry" type jobs. They offered minimal pay, few benefits, and even fewer career possibilities. This meant that inmates on release weren't getting any real help in terms of their futures. And with expenses being what they were (lodging, food, travel, cigarettes, an occasional soda or coffee on break, etc.), it was almost impossible for inmates to save any money. It really wasn't much of a program as it turned out, but it was better than nothing. And, as I was to find out with other rehabilitative programs, this was a standard that most everyone involved would have to settle for. So our better-than-nothing program was deemed a success, and, importantly for me, this helped in establishing the credibility of Terry and my work-related abilities.

Terry had other responsibilities as well. He was a unit counselor, which meant that inmates were in and out of our office daily, discussing problems or making certain requests. In almost all instances, the inmates wanted me present at the discussions, as I represented one of them and I would usually help persuade Terry to act on their behalf. Terry also liked the idea of having someone like me close to his process, as I had gained the respect of the inmates given my education program and my position in the work-release office. In simple terms, I found myself in a good spot.

Another of Terry's responsibilities served to increase his power (and mine) in the facility. He determined what other inmates would be chosen to make the trip from the northern facility to Jean. As his assistant, he allowed me to suggest possible candidates because I knew many of the potential choices. I, of course, suggested my old pals, Jughead and Hazen, as well as several others, and it wasn't more than three months before they joined me at SNCC.

It was almost like an old-home week when we met on the yard and we quickly formed the most powerful "clique" at the new facility. Interestingly, it wasn't the typical clique, based on fear and extortion, although we developed such power. Instead, our power came from getting things done with minimal conflict or confrontation, from using logic in an arbitration-like fashion to dissolve problems that were occurring. We had a small facility, with easy access to an open administration, and being black or Hispanic or white didn't seem to matter that much. Although we all knew that it wouldn't always be that way, that as the place got more crowded and the typical inmate population settled in (remember, a good number of the inmates at this point had been almost hand-picked) the usual prison atmosphere would follow. I was hoping, however, that through my educational successes, I could get out in time to beat that clock.

With my education program in full swing, my job responsibilities as they were and my yard associations intact, I developed a regular, day-to-day routine. After breakfast with Jughead and Hazen, I would go to the work-release office and make the morning coffee. As I awaited Terry's arrival, I would try to get my job-related duties—filing, typing, sorting out inmate problem notes or requests and so on—completed or at least underway. By mid-morning, I would usually find myself caught up with the day's work, which would then allow me time to work on my academic assignments. Terry was as amenable to this schedule as a boss could be, and he tried to provide me with as much time with my studies as possible. He would even do my work at times to make sure I attended to my educational demands. At lunchtime, I would again meet my friends and we would eat together while chatting about what was happening on the yard, or what might be bothering any one of us in terms of our personal problems. We would then hangout in front of the barbershop or gym for an hour or so, oftentimes playing cards to pass the time until we returned to our designated jobs. I would then return to my half-job, half-educational program duties until dinner-time, when the meeting process would again occur.

Almost always, I would stay on the yard after dinner for only an hour. We would usually walk around the track that surrounded the ball field, stopping to talk with other inmates as we passed them by. After this bit of exercise I would then return to my room, one now filled with books and papers, and at times the typewriter that Terry would allow me to borrow for a night's work. I would attend to my reading and writing, only on occasion getting involved in a card game, watching television or playing ball. (I did manage to organize and play on the championship baseball team, along with my old "chain-mates," J.T. and George.) These diversions usually occurred on the weekends, as did my Saturday and Sunday afternoon visits. On those days my girlfriend would come for three or four hours, and, every so often, an old friend or two would stop by for a visit.

Visiting, as was noted earlier, was an important feature of prison life, usually bringing happiness at a visitor's arrival and depression upon departure. These feelings, of course, are common with almost all type visits, whether it comes with family outings, seeing old friends or what have you. But the process of visiting in prison was, as might be suspected, very different.

Each visitor had to be cleared by the prison administration, as they attempted to screen out crime associates or people of suspicious backgrounds. This was difficult, because potential visitors were often best friends or even relatives who were also former crime partners. These individuals would therefore be denied visits, or only allowed to visit via the booth (individuals-on-a-phone-looking-through-the-glass-screen process). For inmates and visitors alike, these possibilities were problematic. (At SNCC, despite her already being cleared at the northern facility, my girlfriend and I started out with this phone-glass visit. This happened on her first visit because a correctional officer made the decision that we were former crime partners. This lasted only for one month, until we again received clearance for contact visits, but the experience of being "denied" was a difficult one.)

Acceptable visitors had to wait in line to be cleared by the guard staff. This meant that each individual had to be signed in, and any gifts, packages or purses they carried would be set aside for a possible search. Occasionally, a visitor would be personally searched, which required that that person, escorted by a same-sex guard into a private room, be stripped and searched. This was not common, usually happening when a guard suspected some type of smuggling operation. But, it could also occur when a guard simply had a "hard-on" for a certain inmate, deciding to take this feeling out on the inmate's visitor. In either case, the experience for the visitor was not a welcomed one. Once cleared and inspected, however, visitors would then proceed to a visiting area to await their inmate counterpart.

Inmates were allowed to proceed to the visiting center once they received a call in their unit announcing a visitor. Most of us knew when a visitor was expected and we would prepare ourselves, especially if it was a girlfriend or a wife, in what was considered our best, or a least most clean, attire. (We were allowed several shirts or sweaters were to be sent to us and they provided a variation to the prison jean shirts.) We would sit in the unit, trying to act as unconcerned about the visit as possible, but everyone was anxiously awaiting the call announcing a visitor. On occasion, a visitor would not arrive on the expected day, and the inmate would end up feeling quite foolish and angry over his preparations. There were also inmates who had no visitors at all. In each case, the situation was troublesome to the inmate. But, like so many other things, it was recognized as simply a part of the prison process.

The same recognition held true for the strip searches that occurred both coming and going from visits. The visiting area was one of the places, but certainly not the only one, where drugs, money or other contraband could be exchanged. "Green" or real money is prized in prison, primarily because it can't be traced like the money that is put on an inmate's account book. Therefore, an inmate might be strip searched on his way into a visit, generally to prevent him from sending out money, an illegal correspondence or something he stole from another inmate, and was almost always strip searched at the end of a visit. The process was a bit dehumanizing, for the guards as well as the inmates. One was asked to completely strip, and then after hair and mouth were inspected, to bend over, spread the buttocks, then lift the genitals, all while the guard looked you over. Again, it became an acceptable part of the visiting process, but it always evoked a contemptuous feeling, especially if one had a difficult or strained visit. (Prison life was filled with these kinds of circumstances, "prison paradoxes" if you will. They occur primarily as security issues "rub up against" human feelings. It's easy, particularly for those on the outside, to believe that whatever needs to be done in a prison to maintain security and control ought to be done. Inmates themselves, at least the "real con" type, generally subscribe to this thought as well. But a good number of these type measures lend themselves to obtrusive and offensive actions, only making the inmate feel less connected to any piece of the social fabric. If the inmate already feels that he has little, if any, stake in society to begin with, then simple intuition tells you that further dehumanization only causes anger. One may think that this is also fine, that this is what inmates deserve. Or, one may think that this experience should keep an inmate from coming back to prison. Although I tend to disagree, the former may be a fair assessment. The latter, however, is simply off the mark. Humiliation confuses and angers already confused and angry people. It is a good portion of the reason why so many individuals, an alarming 70 percent, get out of prison, harm again and then return.)

The visiting, my job, sports, everything, was overshadowed by my education program. I became a political science major, and I was immersed in books that talked about the United States as an experiment in democracy, as well as books that were critical of a "capitalist" America. The more I read, the more I was swayed by the latter, especially given what my environment suggested. I worked very hard through the term, and I was rewarded with straight As. I would again have to apply to the classification committee for the next term's enrollment, but I was adopting the feeling that the process was becoming a mere formality. It turned out to be just that, as the committee, again with the captain and program director objecting, approved my request for another term, but denied, with some deliberation this time, the possibility of actually attending any classes.

There was something else occurring, however, that didn't fit with the success of my education program. This something was actually inconsistent with what my goals appeared to be, something that could support what the captain and program director had implied with their "he's just getting over on the system" attitudes. This something could totally alter my "mere formality" relationship with the classification committee. And, this something certainly deserves note.

As you might recall, when I was in the northern facility beginning my quest for an education program, I stayed involved with the inmate lifestyle primarily because I feared that an education program would never materialize. This meant that I was continuing to push for a program (staying in the "academic camp") while integrating myself into the power hierarchy of the prison world (staying in the "inmate camp"). This foot-in-each-camp balance continued when I got to SNCC, as I was getting more involved with my educational program, while I was also part of the developing inmate power group.

I was fully aware of the "luck–God" inspired fortune I had encountered up to this point, and one would think that, given this awareness, I would be totally convinced to stay as far away from any potential trouble as I could. But, even to my surprise, this was not something that would actually occur.

While I was indeed focused on my academic work, my inmate camp interests prompted an involvement with what I now refer to as post-prison scheming. What I mean is that during my time at SNCC, I continued to discuss with other inmates, in particular the most powerful black and biker inmates, the possibility of organizing an association from which we could control most of the drug business, and all the activities that surround that business, in Las Vegas. Usually outside of the chow hall or the barbershop, a small group of us would occasionally and cautiously meet, agreeing that once we all got out (which was very likely to happen within close proximity to each other), we would organize ourselves into the association, with each leader responsible for certain activities. The black leaders would handle the distribution, the bikers would provide the muscle, and I would be responsible for supplying the best and least expensive drug products. We also all agreed that the money and power generated from our work would be split into equal shares.

Obviously, this planning was not consistent with my academic goals. And, as mentioned, it was equally inconsistent with the good fortune that had gotten me to the position I was in. Yet, I participated in this scheming despite it being illogical. I couldn't put my finger on exactly why I needed to be involved with such risky behavior, but I honestly looked forward to our meetings and liked the idea that I still had at least one foot firmly planted in the inmate camp.

And this wasn't the only risk-taking, foot-in-the-inmate-camp behavior I was involved with. On occasion, I would get high on marijuana, sometimes in combination with our prison-made wine, pruno. I would almost always end up feeling extremely paranoid about this, sensing that my different behavior would attract the eye of a correctional officer who could then ask me to submit to a urine test. If I failed the test, my probation could be revoked (remember I was on probation simultaneous to my prison sentence), and my education program would be all but finished. In other words, with the potential of gaining more time and losing my education program, I had a lot on the line. Nevertheless, I continued the behavior, keeping my foot in that camp, despite the possible outcome.

The most alarming experience I had being high occurred in my room one evening as I was sharing a joint of newly arrived pot with a fellow inmate. There was a strict rule that no inmate should be in another's cell, but Fat Jack had persuaded me that a few hits of this great stuff would only take a second's time. I was in a celebratory mood because I had just received some positive news about my education program, so there we were, smoking pot in my room. Within that second's time I heard the footsteps of a guard coming up the stairs toward my door and I turned cold. Jack dove under my bunk against the far wall and pulled the blanket down to the floor so the officer couldn't tell anyone was there. I immediately turned on my hot water (which, in our unit, came on almost instantly) to let some steam rise, to clear the air of the pot smell and smoke, and I lit a cigarette to camouflage our activity. The guard arrived at my door and peered in seeming to know exactly what was going on. My heart was pounding so hard that I thought it would pop out into his face as I asked him what was up. He said "you tell me," and as I started to explain that the steam would help my sinus condition, he was called down to the unit office for some other business. He walked away with a suspicious look on his face, and as he did so, Fat Jack scurried out the door to the tier and on down to his own room. My body seemed to catch the bed as I lay motionless, stunned and dizzy.

It was luck, pure and simple, that I wasn't at that moment in handcuffs, awaiting some form of processing that would take away everything I had worked so hard to achieve. How could I do this, I thought? What was I thinking? I must be crazy! Perhaps I was. I was honestly perplexed by my reckless behavior. Yet, I continued to put myself in precarious situations, even, as you will read, when I was back on the outside. It would take awhile, but I would come to understand that the transition from illegitimate to legitimate demanded, as does its reverse, attention to many factors. It would not occur simply as a result of getting into an education program. The process of making a change, to the extent it's actually possible, takes time...and not necessarily the type of time that comes with going to prison. So, my time continued, inmate and student, criminal and academic, a foot in each camp. I finished the term with four As and one B, and I was now a respected member of the university community. But as for my prison membership, I was becoming more angry with every book I read. The doubts raised at the beginning of my studies regarding the Marxist analysis, particularly those pertaining to indoctrination, had all but disappeared. I was convinced of the merits of the analysis and I was, in fact, moving the interpretations of my own criminal behavior from the "money is the root of all evil" idea to more circumspect considerations.

Looking back through my younger years, I was coming to think that my connection to the "money/profit over all else" idea was influenced by the booming, capitalist fifties America, especially with its relationship to the development of organized crime, both of which played out in my neighborhood. I could also see a connection to crime and the feeling of freedom in the fifties and sixties, as well as the disparate and confusing gap between what America was supposed to be; free, equal, just, fair, etc., and what the Civil Rights Movement and Vietnam War exposed us to be. It seemed to me that this combination of things fueled, in an almost osmotic way, a sense of reckless indifference toward what was socially or politically acceptable, a sense which I now perceived as an important ingredient relative to understanding my criminal behavior. To the point, I was learning that to understand one's behavior, one had to develop a clear and accurate understanding of political and economic history.

Most of what I was now reading was particular to a Marxist, radical, critical analysis of capitalism. For my political science courses I was reading a great deal about how the economic determinates of capitalism tended to consume even the most powerful political ideals. This was indeed a troubling notion. And, in terms of my criminal justice and sociology courses, I was reading about how this occurrence at the economic and political levels was causing and perpetuating crime and the other social problems evident in America. This was no less troublesome.

At times, particularly after reading how exploitive and oppressive a capitalist system could be and how alternatives to it existed, I would feel overwhelmed with anger. My feelings were strong and passionate and I would think of taking to the soap box to encourage dissent, even revolt. I wanted to shout out to my fellow inmates, telling them that they were part of a class whose under-educated, under-skilled and under-employed lot in life was primarily the result of a system designed around the ideas of competition and profit. It was a system where access to real avenues of opportunity were almost always limited to those already able to compete. We inmates were part of the "surplus" in this system. We were people who could be used for labor-related ends, filling the lower-paying jobs, serving as potential workers to threaten those in the work force who demanded too much, and comprising a group that provided jobs for others who had to tend to us. Unfortunately, we were also part of an entire class of people who had little control over these ends.

Of course, I had my probationary sentence hanging over my head so this type of speech making would indeed be dangerous. But of equal importance was that, even though most of those housed at SNCC came from the disadvantaged circumstances that spoke directly to a Marxist interpretation, the facility itself was not so bad. It was new, everyone had a job and even the food was decent. It did, in fact, create a sense of complacency among the inmates. So, as angry as I was, I could imagine that given this complacency, and given what I had been allowed to do while in prison, my criticisms would fall on deaf ears or people would wonder what all my hollering was about. In short, it was neither the time nor place for such a demonstration.

This complacency dilemma would manifest itself in a different way once I got out of prison. As my being a successful and well-educated person began to overshadow my crime-to-prison experiences, people would ask, "Why should you be so angry or upset with the system?" "Isn't this, after all, the best system in the world?" "Why aren't you enjoying what the system has to offer?" "Why don't you take advantage of what it has afforded you?"

The insinuation of complacency attached to these questions caused as much anger within me as I experienced while in prison. In fact, I would see it as an actual part of our problems, especially in light of the enormous difficulties we faced, difficulties that could, unless realistically addressed, cause us to lose what we had been afforded. Unlike in prison, however, I would object as loud as discretion would permit, as I began to feel a sense of responsibility for all that I had learned, as well as for the good fortune that had accompanied my learning it. My objections, of course, in spite of it being a better time and a better place, would create problems of their own.

There was something else occurring at SNCC that angered me, something that put my entire education program in jeopardy. It appeared that our warden, Ed P., had enemies in the Nevada State Prison System, in particular his supervisor, the director of prisons. As I understood it, their animosity stemmed from their differing philosophies about how a prison system should operate. Ed P.'s liberal philosophy was consistent with the plan for SNCC and was the primary reason he was hired. He believed in the rehabilitative model, which, in general terms, relies on the availability of programs and privileges to help turn the inmates into civilized beings. The director believed that this model didn't work, that it was too soft on the inmates. He favored the conservative-oriented, punishment model, where strict rules and constant discipline are the focus and programs and privileges are kept at a minimum. He believed that it was within this type of environment that inmates would learn how to control themselves once back in society. The director had apparently objected to SNCC being built with the alternate philosophy in mind, and so he had it "in" for Ed P. from the beginning of the Jean project.

After almost two years in operation, SNCC was becoming more of a regular prison, with the population up to capacity and the inmates no longer of the selected type. This meant that the normal problems of prison life like gang activity, drug smuggling, sexual batteries, etc., were becoming quite common. The director wanted to exert more control over the inmate population, to batten down the hatches so to speak, before the freedom of the inmates got out of hand. To do this, he would have to get rid of Ed P.

Coincidental to this philosophical difference, a significant amount of money was found missing from the state prison coffers. No one was sure how this happened or who was responsible, but the director, who eventually turned out to be involved, accused Ed P. of having something to do with the situation. With this in-fighting occurring, Ed P. either quit or was fired and a new warden was put in his place. The new warden was a close associate of the director, and this meant that he would support the beliefs and policies of the director as much as possible. In fact, some referred to the new warden as the director's "lackey."

I was angry because this all came to a head about one month before my next classification committee meeting and the new warden (or I should say director) was not supportive of my education program. Saying that the program had not been passed through the proper administrative channels, he was going to veto its existence. When I heard this I could not believe it. To take away a successful education program seemed ludicrous, despite any philosophical differences. I was outraged by this possibility. Yet, this circumstance taught me a great deal about the power of philosophical differences, and it helped to further crystallize my understanding of liberal and conservative politics. Additionally, it made me again consider my good fortune-- what if the director's views had been in place when I arrived at Jean?

I began to gather my supporters, from Randy and the others at the university, to a state senator that my ex-lawyer had put me in touch with, to the administrators at SNCC like Terry, the psych and Father Barry. I asked for letters of support from most of these people, and I got them. I knew if the director recognized that a significant number of people were supportive of the program, people who could, especially from the outside, question his motives for erasing it, he might think twice before allowing his new warden to let that happen.

The tactic worked. The warden allowed me to put my usual request before the classification committee. He would let them again decide on my future. Although I was satisfied with the decision, I was still not assured of a positive the outcome because the warden, the captain and the program director presented a formidable opposition. At meeting time however, the program director changed his objection (apparently he disliked the philosophical direction of the warden and director more than he disliked me), which helped with the committee's approval of my 18-credit term request. Plus, to my greatest surprise, and perhaps as a reaction to the attempt to mess with a good program, the committee also approved my request to attend classes. I was going to be able to travel, twice a month under escort, to the campus.

I was well into my second year at SNCC and my first parole board was in sight. The committee's decision meant that I was now assured of finishing the term at about the same time of the board meeting. Therefore, I would almost have my degree completed when the meeting time arrived, except for about one more term. I knew I would need as much fire power as I could gather to persuade the board that I should be released, so I was elated with the committee's decision. By the way...if you can believe it...this was the reason for my celebration with Fat Jack!

The third term was clearly going to be the most rewarding. I would now able be to go to the campus. I was going to be on the outside, free again to see people in their everyday doings. I was very excited about it all.

On my first two trips I was escorted by a correctional officer, a uniformed guard, who was responsible for keeping me in his sight. This meant that he would accompany me wherever I went, staying with me in the classes I attended and waiting outside the door of any professor I might speak with. He was, so to speak, my shadow. I was, of course, happy to be able to do what I was doing so I didn't mind his company. I knew it looked a bit strange, but the attention we drew really wasn't bothersome.

After the first two trips, Terry decided that he would become my escort. Accordingly, we began to schedule the trips to coincide with days he would have to be in the city. And his being my escort changed my days at the school considerably. We would drive to the campus and Terry would designate a place and time for me to meet him. He would then let me go on my own, usually returning in several hours. He took an incredible risk by doing this. I could have run away, or tried to meet some of my old partners or girlfriends, or attempted to get drugs to smuggle. I could have gotten high or drunk, or I could have even committed another crime. But, we knew each other very well and he treated me, and trusted me, like he would a good friend. This treatment continued on our trips back to the facility when he would take me to a restaurant where we would talk over what I had done or thought about at the school. I was very fortunate in having Terry as a friend.

Another major event happened during this period, which coincided with my school-trip opportunities. In conjunction with a vacation in Arizona, my parents, to whom I had been writing and calling on a regular basis, decided to make a stop to visit me at SNCC. I was going to get to see and feel my parents for the first time in awhile, and I was both nervous and excited. A lot had happened since we last saw each other.

On the first day we met at the prison, during visiting hours. It was as emotional an afternoon as I'd ever had. When I walked into the visiting room and saw my parents, I almost fainted. My mother came to me and we hugged. It was a hug I had read about in books and that I had seen portrayed on the screen. It was intense, and although it lasted only a moment, it was filled with a meaning that related the story of a mother and her son. I would never forget that moment.

My father looked great and we embraced as fathers and sons often do, translating that strange mixture of manliness and love as best we could. I was just so happy to see him, with my mother, excited as they were, healthy as they were. We sat and talked about all the things that had been occurring and we laughed and cried over a lot of it. I introduced them to several of my inmate friends, and I remember how polite everyone seemed with each other. My mother, perhaps making a likeness to her son, found it hard to believe that these men were as bad as their crimes would indicate. We had a terrific visit that day. And what made it even better was that Terry had arranged my next school trip the following day, which meant that I could meet with my parents, on their last day in Nevada, on the campus grounds. This also turned out to be a beautiful day. We had a picnic of sorts, and most importantly, we got to see each other in a setting that was much more conducive to a pleasant memory than was SNCC. The two visits provided a tremendous lift to my spirits.

In addition to my parents' visit, I had another uplifting experience that related to my academic endeavors. Toward the close of the term, while in one of my political science courses, I was told that I was being recommended for induction into the National Political Science Honor Society. I had never really considered my work in terms of academic honors so I was surprised by this. And, I was even more surprised when my following visit, the last one I would make, included an induction ceremony with me as one of the new members. I was excited as I received my member certificate. It verified the hard work I had done. Moreover, I imagined that the certificate, along with the five As and one B I received that semester, would be the perfect antidote for any of the negatives that might appear in my upcoming parole board deliberations.

After more than two years in the system, I was now entering into the parole board phase. This phase usually begins about two or three months prior to one's actual meeting date, with board meetings scheduled every month. Meanwhile, the reality of getting out of prison makes itself more clear. It is a time when most inmates begin to concern themselves with getting some type of employment guarantee and when they begin to ask for letters from family members and people in the community to demonstrate a sense of support for their release. Inmates generally become more reserved with their behavior and try to persuade everyone that they are indeed ready to be let go. I had seen other inmates deal with the pressures of this phase, as our work-release office was pivotal to the parole board proceedings. This happened because inmates needed to develop potential work opportunities through our office, and because Terry's duties as a counselor included pre-parole board meeting advice. So, as my time approached, I knew pretty much what to expect.

My worries focused mainly on what the parole board might consider about the time I had served compared to the crimes I had committed. This was going to be my first meeting, and although I had an impressive resume, I knew that the outcome of the meeting was by no means a sure bet.

Terry's input was important at this time as he continually cautioned me about what I should or shouldn't do at the meeting. In many of our academic discussions I had become quite strong in my sentiments about what I saw happening in the prison systems in the country. I saw them as nothing more than very expensive warehouses, as neither punishment nor rehabilitation attempts were working. Terry warned me not to allow myself to be pushed to that level of excitement during the meeting. He was also aware that I had some radical ideas on how the system might be changed. For example, I had become an advocate for the legalization of drugs like heroin, cocaine and marijuana. I felt that taking the profit out of the supply, demand and profit equation, coupled with making drug abuse a medical/health issue instead of a criminal justice one, seemed a more logical way to address the drug problem. He suggested that I stay away from mentioning any of these ideas at the meeting. He wanted me to be politically correct with the board, to tell them what they wanted to hear.

With my freedom in the balance, this seemed like a common-sense approach. Yet, I had a hard time accepting it. In fact, it was pretty much at this juncture that I began to think about how difficult being a radical could be. I believed that there was something wrong with the system on all levels, yet I had to compromise my beliefs to get what I needed. I wasn't happy about this. But, I soothed the realization by thinking that this was only a temporary compromise and that I needed to get out of the system before I could involve myself with changing it. It seemed clear that I had to be on the outside to make change happen, although I had no idea how difficult the outside would be.

I was the third inmate to be seen on the parole board meeting day. It was about 10 o'clock in the morning, and I was very nervous. Both inmates before me had received paroles, and when I walked into the meeting room I was thinking about the three-in-a-row odds. The three members of the parole board introduced themselves to me and two of them began asking me a variety of questions about my crimes, my past, my stay in prison and my education program. The third member never asked me a question, but removed his glasses and stared at me while I responded to the others. I found this more than odd, and even though it irritated me, which I assumed was his objective, I decided not to inquire about his behavior.

It was clear to me that the board was not facing an easy decision. They were very impressed with my education program. It was indeed a first for them. I had also been a model inmate, working hard at my job and helping both the staff and other inmates when I could. Terry had been sure to put a letter in my file to that effect.

But, as I suspected, they noted that whatever I had accomplished had to be juxtaposed to the crimes for which I was imprisoned. They were serious offenses, and because I was a rather successful profiteer in the drug business, I could ostensibly be held accountable for a good number of other offenses committed in pursuit of drugs and drug money. I remember wanting to comment on my preference for legalization, asking them if the current drug policy could ostensibly be held accountable for all of us actually being there. I recalled Terry's words however, realizing that it was not a good time for cross examination.

They also noted that they had several letters in my file from the police and the district attorney's office supporting the idea that I should complete a significant portion of my 10-year prison sentence. I could only respond to their points by again noting what I had accomplished, all of which suggested to them that I was ready for release. I also told them that, should I be granted parole, I would finish my undergraduate degree and proceed on to graduate or law school while I worked in the criminal justice field. I pointed out that my ability to handle both work and school had already been demonstrated with what I had done at SNCC. With this point acknowledged, they asked me to leave the room while they deliberated over my potential release.

After about five, very long minutes, I was called back into the room. It was common knowledge that if one made a parole, there would be three copies of a release form on the table. If one did not make a parole, only one denial sheet would be present. I immediately saw the three sheets, and was instantaneously the happiest man in the world. I listened intently as they told me that I would be released in 60 days and that, under the rules of the work-release program, I could attend school daily during that period. I was also given notice that the actual conditions of my parole (i.e., what I could and couldn't do while on parole), would be forthcoming from a soon-to-be-assigned parole officer. I was then given a copy of my release document and told to return to my unit. I thanked them all, even the man who did the staring, and I left, relieved of the pressures I felt when I came.

After over three years of bail, jail and prison, I was now only two months away from my release. It was a conditional release, meaning I would be on parole and subject to rules pertaining to visits with a parole officer, urine testing and close supervision of my behavior. But, I recognized none of the rules as problematic. What I did find problematic, however, was the behavior of the director of prisons, who was now denying my release to attend school.

The reason the director had gotten involved with what the parole board had granted me appeared more vindictive than anything else. The board had granted me the opportunity to attend school under the work-release provision of the law. The law was clear that an educational release could be issued within its guidelines, but apparently no one had actually exercised that right until now. The director, who I believed was still stinging over what had happened previously, decided that because it had never occurred in the past, it was not going to occur at all, despite what the law said.

Terry and I were very upset over the director's misinterpretation of the law, and his misuse of power as well. I had little time for the next term's enrollment and I knew it would take some time to change his mind, if this was at all possible. I addressed a letter to his office, including a copy of the statute that clearly indicated that an educational release was in the context of the work-release language. I also indicated that the parole board had already made a decision, one that was actually theirs to make. I received no reply.

I then heard that the director was to be at SNCC for some type of ceremony, and I decided I would confront him with copies of what had been addressed to his office. In the chow hall, as he sat with a number of his cronies, I approached his table with my inquiry. I was nervous and angry. When I introduced myself, the director quickly said, "I know who you are. What do you want?" My anger level went up a notch, but I calmed myself and asked him if he would look at the information that would warrant my educational release. He took the papers and with only a cursory review, responded, "Palombo, if you wanted a fucking education, you should have stayed out of fucking prison!"

I stood there, frozen for several moments. I had violent thoughts, and I felt like hitting him as hard as I could. He even had a look on his face that seemed to challenge me to do just that. I sensed that the other inmates around expected something to happen, but I turned away, shaking inside. I returned to my table and sat with my friends, each one patting me on the back, implying I did the right thing. I was furious, but I knew what I had done was what should have been done. I had too much to lose at that point.

As I talked with Terry about the incident, he gave me the kind of advice I had become accustomed to. I should forget about the release, enroll for nine credits for the term, help him train a new work-release clerk and get myself prepared for a new life. It was time to relax a bit.

And so I did just that. I spent a lot of time thinking about what had happened over the past several years. Changes had occurred within me, but I wasn't sure to what extent I was a changed person. I would definitely find out more about this once I was back on the outside. I did know one thing for certain, however. I was one fortunate being. I doubted whether the streak of good luck I had encountered, no matter how much I might pray, could ever happen again.

At the end of the 60 days, I said my good-byes to the people I had come to know quite well. I gathered my box of personals, my prison "diploma" and my two hundred, state-issued, road-money dollars, and I walked out the gate...out of a place I knew was changing, out of a place I would hope to never return.

As a postscript to the chapter, I should mention that the educational process I had organized was closed off to other inmates after I left. I got out, perhaps just in time.

PART TWO

Chapter 5

RE-ADJUSTING

I had heard about the possibilities of culture shock, but I dismissed them, feeling that I would adjust rather quickly to the outside world. I hadn't been locked up so long, and I had been on the outside occasionally during my time of incarceration, so what was there to be shocked about? It didn't take me long to realize, however, that I was indeed affected by being back in the "normal" world. Some might argue that Las Vegas is hardly normal, but that is another story.

I was no longer living in a routine, controlled environment, where everyone was pretty much involved with the same processes. Instead, people on the outside had a wide variety of agendas, some of which conflicted in what seemed like unruly ways with what I needed to do. It appeared to me that people on the outside were actually more rude, pushy and insensitive than those on the inside, especially when they were in lines or when they were driving. I found this very annoying and several times I felt like punching the people around me when they had no sympathy at all for me or anyone else who was just trying to do what needed to be done.

I didn't like this feeling at all, and it caused me at times to want to get away from people, totally away from the discomfort they seemed to cause. I realized, of course, that people had always acted this way, and that I had been one who regularly participated in this type of behavior as well. I simply never recognized how offensive it could feel until now, and I wasn't sure whether I should just take time getting reintegrated into accepting and participating in the behavior again, or whether I should move away from it all. In the first several months after my release it seemed I was always uncomfortable around people.

But, I also made myself uncomfortable, primarily because I was really a different person than when I had gone into prison. As an example, you might have noticed that I had a good deal of angry moments while in prison. I had always recognized this characteristic as macho and positive, a temper not to be pushed. But now my anger, which was still with me, represented something I wasn't comfortable with, something I wanted to be less a part of, something I knew I would have to work at even though I was still angry with what I saw happening around me.

I had undergone a metamorphosis of sorts, but I was still walking around without really knowing a great deal about my new self or where this new self would take me. I didn't have it so bad though. I often thought about what it would be like if I had been in prison for a longer time, or if, on getting out, I had little promise for future legitimate endeavors, or no strong family and friend support. Given the power of the uneasiness I felt, any one of these ifs, and especially a combination of all three, would have certainly made it easier to slip back into anti-social behavior, the consequences of which would be a return to prison. This, by the way, is the result for many who are released without much more than the clothes on their back. Fortunately, and I'm sure you're beginning to understand what I mean with this word, I had things happening that helped to keep me from this fate.

The place where I felt most comfortable was at the university. When I was released I was enrolled in a nine-credit term and I decided to also take the law school admission tests (LSATs), thinking that I might want to become a lawyer. I did well with my coursework (three As) and I did well on the LSATs. I had now come to see myself as being a full and legitimate part of the academic community. I was learning a great deal while there, but I also felt that through sharing my experiences I was contributing to the learning process of others. The recognition of this exchange helped me tremendously, as it fed the realization of my own worth. Simply put, I liked the idea that I could help others.

While finishing school, I was receiving additional support with the "learning how to help others" idea. Father Barry, whom I had become friends with while incarcerated, (and who, in addition to being very good at his profession, had a strong understanding of the Marxist analysis) was interested in developing a program for the growing, yet unattended to offender and ex-offender population in Southern Nevada. We had briefly discussed this possibility while I was still at SNCC and I was as interested as he was in making such a project a reality.

Upon my release, I visited him at the Franciscan Center in North Las Vegas and he told me that there was a possibility that we could secure a small grant from his Franciscan Brotherhood specifically to develop a program. With this seed money we could create a position for a program director/co-founder/developer, and he was hoping that I could fill that role. I was very excited about this prospect. It would give me the chance to work at a job (something I sorely needed) where I could exercise my desire to help other people. Within a month's time of his asking, we were issued funds to organize our ideas into state and federal government grant form.

The project was named Nexus, and although the work was tiresome and detailed, I learned a great deal about the grant-writing process. What I most enjoyed about my work was being the program spokesperson. In this role I was responsible for going out into the community to talk with leaders from the church, the schools, the police and sheriff departments and other state and county agencies to persuade them to support our program. I enjoyed this process enormously as I talked with a variety of people, all of whom had a variety of thoughts on what needed to be done with the crime problem, about a project I felt very strongly about. The fact that the prison population was growing in Nevada, and that there were no stable projects addressing the concerns we intended to address (pre-and post-release counseling on issues ranging from controlling violent behavior to finding and keeping work), and that we were asking for verbal not monetary support from the people and agencies, made my work a bit easier than it might otherwise have been. My endeavors were successful. I received endorsements from everyone I spoke with, and I began to polish my communication skills as well.

This was my first attempt at community work, and my enthusiasm for the project was high. The work was providing me with a valuable sense of direction, but as important as all this was, I was troubled by what we couldn't do with the program. Both Father Barry and I realized that our program could do little in regard to the economic and political changes that we both saw as necessary to address crime-related problems. Simply put, the nature of capitalism, and especially the inherent lack of opportunity for members of the lower class, i.e., most of our proposed clientele, would have to go unattended. After all, it would be foolish to think that government-sponsored agencies would be interested in a project that included ideas about radical changes to the capitalist way of life. Therefore, we had to utilize the vernacular of the day in our project proposals, speaking to the idea that offenders and ex-offenders could become productive, job-holding members of the community, even though we knew that the jobs and opportunities would remain limited, especially in relationship to those we hoped to serve.

It was a repeat of the work-release "better than nothing" scenario, and I didn't really care for it. I was annoyed by thinking about the other programs that had similar realizations. Moreover, this type of self-manipulation--doing things that I knew weren't exactly right, ignoring both means and long-term ends—aroused a sensation similar to that which my criminal activities had elicited. In those days it was all simply a part of the trade. But now, in trying to be on the straight and narrow, recognizing it as part of this trade evoked a sense of contempt. There was little I could do at this point, but I maintained hope that, if I kept at projects like this, if I learned the trade so to speak, that I could make a difference in getting "real" programs that included all the variables that were connected to the American processes off the ground. I wasn't sure how this was going to happen, or how much time it would take, but I felt that it would happen in much the same way it happened with my education plan in prison. I would just keep working at it, and time, I expected and prayed, would help with the rest.

My work with Nexus got combined with another project that had much the same format, except on a larger scale. I was asked to become an occupational essentials instructor in the CETA program operating out of the community college in Las Vegas. Designed under President Johnson's War on Poverty Program, its objectives were to assist lower-income people in getting at least a high school level education, training them in a variety of technical programs and then helping them to locate work. (If a job was available, it would, unfortunately, almost always be of a low-paying, semi-skilled nature.) Incentives were also given to businesses to encourage them to hire program graduates. My role was to help the participants organize their thoughts on all that they were going through, and to help them keep focused on making improvements in their lives.

Here again the program, though an elaborate effort, seemed to be premised on the false reality that jobs and career opportunities existed for the program participants. In fact, most of those I came in contact with realized that their involvement with the program was a temporary respite from a world that wouldn't really change. And this was proven true when the CETA job developer, searching for opportunities for those finishing the program, would only find quality employment for a few. In one instance, the developer found slots for some 30 people at a Vegas resort, all in housekeeping positions. Because no other jobs were available at the time, some of those positions were filled by CETA participants. As the incentives given to the resort for hiring these people were about to run out, all of them were given notice that their jobs were being terminated.

It was clear that such job-market realities, realities that I perceived as tied to the nature of capitalism, were bound to surface, particularly since they weren't addressed from the beginning of the program. In short, the cycle of poverty seemed destined to continue. In fact, a few of my former inmate acquaintances came through the program. Surprised as they were to see me doing what I was doing, we shared some ironic humor about how the same people ended up in the same type programs, myself included. Unfortunately, out of the four, only one obtained a job that promised any future dividends, as a cook in a hotel. And I, not the job developer, arranged for the opportunity.

Suffice it to say, I had the same concerns about the shortcomings of the CETA program that I did about Nexus, and I reacted to them in the same way. I couldn't do much about the larger picture, but I could continue to help people think about their lives and the system, whether a job would materialize for them or not. As with Nexus, this became my focus. I knew I would learn more about social programs, and I felt that when the time came I would be able to utilize my experiences to help make changes. It was a rationalization of my current work, no doubt, but one I believed only of a temporary nature.

This was indeed an interesting, albeit confusing, period in my life. I was completing my long-sought-after college education and working at community projects. I was certainly doing things I never expected to do. And there appeared the potential for me to continue on the same path. But I was also struggling with my new self, trying to understand and actually visualize what this new self was about. What was this ex-drug dealer, ex-con doing anyway? Would people really respect me given my past? Would I have to become the ultimate reformed individual, someone on a moral crusade, a real "do-gooder" to overcome this? Could I become such a person? Did I want to be? And, where would my newly found radical self fit into all this? Would people see this as simply an extension of my criminal/rebel past? And, what did that spell in terms of my future?

Amidst these pushing and pulling feelings was the strong sense that I needed to stay with education. I had more to learn and I realized that only through education could I establish the foundation to make the differences I was hoping to make. Besides, I had already come a long way and I didn't want to go back over that road again.

I also wanted to stay involved in community work. I enjoyed helping people and I felt that it was in the community where changes would actually materialize. In fact, this "foot in each camp" idea mirrored the "one foot in academics and the other in inmate life" situation I found myself in while in prison, and I liked the position. I was trying to convince myself that, whatever I would end up doing, this straddle would be involved. But, something else was happening that was inconsistent with these thoughts...something that could end all my hopes for a future with education and community work. This something was tugging at my "new" person and my "new" direction.

This something was pulling me back almost as if I had no trust in what I was doing or where I was going. It was something that made me wonder whether my feet were as firmly planted where I knew they should be.

If you recall, I had been involved with what I termed "post-prison scheming" while in prison. This related to a plan that entailed my being a member in an association whose focus was to control the drug and related crime activities in Las Vegas. Well, about four months after my release, I spent several evenings with the other individuals who were to be in this association, discussing its possibilities. My prison pals Jughead and Hazen were included in these discussions. We came to the conclusion on those evenings that we could do what we had planned to do. All we needed was to better organize the plan and then implement it.

Although I didn't hesitate to participate in the meetings, I was not at all convinced that I wanted to follow through with the plan. It was clearly at odds with everything else I was doing and saying, and I was now actually a bit scared of the whole idea. I told my associates about my ambivalence. Even though they respected what I had done, and was doing, with education, they seemed to think or hope that it was simply a matter of time before I changed my mind. They thought I would eventually "see the light" and commit to making the plan happen. I was never sure at that time why I was staying involved with the plan. I sensed it was a mixture of things—my new freedom, the lure of the excitement of crime, money and power, my wish to keep my word about doing what I said I would do, and even my uncertainty about what my future might be like, especially given the contradictions I was seeing develop in my legitimate experiences. Whatever the reasons, I stayed involved with the plan.

One evening, after a get together about the plan, I was drinking quite heavily with some of my old friends in a club notorious for being a "mob joint." The place was managed by one of these friends and I mentioned to him our plan to take over the action in Vegas. He was a bit surprised by this, as he was aware of my other activities, but, he seemed to recognize the plan's potential. He suggested that given the seriousness of such an undertaking, I speak with the "boss of Vegas" before I actually made any real moves.

It was about two in the morning and the club was crowded with card and dice dealers, show girls, gamblers, mob guys and quasi-mob guys. This atmosphere, the alcohol and being with my "partners" all seemed to volcanically come together when I heard my manager friend's suggestion. I raised my voice to a fairly high level as I told him that I didn't need to talk with anyone to do what I wanted to do. I had the cooperation of the kind of people who could make the plan happen and any one else's approval was not necessary. I reinforced my position with the comment that if the big boss thought that a problem existed, I would meet him anywhere, preferably in a phone booth, where he and I alone could fight it out. As far as I was concerned, it could be kill or be killed.

This made my manager friend very nervous since the club he was in charge of, the club we were in, was actually owned by the boss. He said again that it would be best if I talked with the boss, and he also remarked that I should be careful about what I was suggesting. I half-heartedly laughed this off as we returned to our drinks. At that moment an older man stopped at my barstool and looked directly into my eyes. He gave me a look I had seen before, that "red light blinking at a railroad crossing" type look, accompanied by a light pat on my cheek. I knew immediately that this was a warning from somebody who knew about warnings and that I was being told that my words were putting me into a dangerous situation. The older man turned and walked out of the bar without a word. I remember feeling the significance of this little interlude, but I brushed it aside as my friends and I carried on. The impact of this night would not be known until several days later.

The next day I was not at all happy with myself. I didn't like what I had said at the bar. I never liked loud mouths and I didn't feel at all comfortable with the direction my words had taken me. However, I decided to let my doubts rest. I had done what I had done. I would put my trust in the hands of the "god-luck-fate" combination that had gotten me this far and let happen whatever was going to happen. What else could I do?

A few nights later I returned to the club with a friend of mine. As we sat at the bar and chatted, a man came up and sat at the stool next to mine. I thought this a bit peculiar as there were several other stools available, but I tried to ignore his presence. After a few minutes, the man offered to buy us a drink. I felt uncomfortable with the offer and told him that we were about to leave but thanks anyway. He then placed his hand on my arm and with a squeeze insisted that we have a drink. I was annoyed by his behavior, but I said okay and, in a manner that expressed a certain sense of bravado, I extended my hand to introduce myself. He shook my hand, telling me that he knew whom I was, and he then introduced himself. I recognized his name immediately, he was the boss of Las Vegas. (Actually, Tony S. represented the mob's interest in Las Vegas, and had attained his position based mainly on his reputation for being a tough guy and a killer.)

I reacted at first by looking at my friend who was clearly shaken by the situation. With the boss's hand still in mine, I quickly glanced around the bar and noticed that everyone had left, save three or four large men who were sitting at a table directly behind us. And, I knew they were his guys. I was in no way sure what direction our conversation would turn, but I said to him that I was happy to meet him in person because I had some things to tell him. He responded that he had heard that I had things to say and he suggested that we talk about "these things."

I was a bit dazed by the circumstance, as anything could have happened. He could have killed me and my friend right there, or just decided to beat us half to death. But, I remained as cool as I could and began to explain the plan to take over the drug activities in Vegas. He listened to the ideas without saying a word. When I finished, he looked at me and shook his head in a bewildered way. He began to tell me about all his problems with federal agents, state authorities, the IRS and the mob itself. He told me that he wished he could have done something else with his life, something that would not have put him in the situation he was in.

Why, he asked, would a guy like me, someone who had recently been in prison, yet had gotten an education and was on his way to doing other things be interested in getting back into activities that promised nothing but trouble? Why wasn't I smart enough to move on?

I was in a state of semi–shock. I wasn't expecting any of this type conversation to happen. I was surprised he knew so much about me, and I had no idea how to answer his question. I sort of shrugged my shoulders feeling like a schoolboy being confronted by the teacher. He then told me that I could do whatever I decided to do. If I decided to follow through with the proposed plan, we would let the chips fall where they may. I took this to mean that he wouldn't commit to doing anything at his point, either for or against the plan. But, he suggested, I should seriously think about the alternative, because it might be my last chance to get away from a less-than-promising future.

He left his stool and returned to his associates at the table. I swallowed the last bit of my drink and with a nod to my friend we got up to leave. I looked over my shoulder and said good night to the boss and we walked out the door. I was still nervous as we got into the car wondering if someone was lying in wait for us, but nothing happened. As we drove home I thought of the different things that could have occurred, and what actually happened. I didn't know why this extremely dangerous man acted the way he did. Was he leery of the power that our "association" represented? Did he really like our plan and was he just testing me out? Did he think I was working with the police? Was he under someone else's surveillance? Or, did he think he would take this one occasion to turn a good deed? Whatever the reason, I knew it was highly unlikely that what had happened would happen again. The next time things would surely be different!

The following morning the boss's words were fresh in my mind. I knew I could no longer play the game I was playing, this half good guy, half bad-guy routine. I would have to make a decision and make it quickly. I thought again about his remarks. The mobster made sense. Why wasn't I smart enough to move on?

In that afternoon's mail, that same afternoon mind you, I received an important letter. It was from the law school I had applied to in California. They had reviewed my grades and my admission tests and had decided to accept me. It was a late acceptance, evidently there had been some deliberation over allowing a person with my past into the school, and I had to respond as soon as possible regarding my intentions. I must have sat there with that letter in my hand for an hour. I was at a crossroads in my life, and this letter was most assuredly a sign pointing to what direction I should take. I could hardly believe that things happened this way, but they did.

I set out the following day to get my affairs in order. I telephoned the school to let them know that I was on my way, notified both Father Barry and the CETA program that I was about to leave and reported to the parole office to request an interstate compact that would allow me to move to another state. And, I also had to tell my association partners that I was now out of the plan.

It took me several weeks to get everything organized. When I was done, I packed my car and headed for Sacramento, California... where my next life would begin to unfold.

PART THREE

Chapter 6

ACADEMIC CONCERNS

I arrived in Sacramento with great expectations. Although I was now 30 years old, I did have a college education—I had graduated with high honors and membership in the National Political Science Honor Society—and a good deal of experience in life and with the system I wanted to change. I knew there would be difficulties in addressing those changes. But by separating myself from the dangerous lifestyle I had left behind, and remembering all the good fortune I had experienced, and having the potential to become a lawyer and raise my power base, I had reason enough to be hopeful.

I hoped to become a lawyer so my comments on the political, economic and social issues that concerned me would carry more weight, which in turn would help me create greater change. And, for some reason, though no one actually told me this, I convinced myself that law school would lend itself to a better understanding of those issues. In other words, I was focused more on the idea of being a lawyer than on what I was going to have to learn and do to become one. I found out relatively quickly that the law school process was not what I wanted it to be.

For me, the course work was dull, tedious and clearly not directed at the political, economic and social variables I wanted to concentrate on. It focused on the theory of the law, with almost no thought of how the law was actually practiced. I had seen it in motion and it was not a pretty sight. I would often sit in the classroom and shake my head in dismay as the class struggled over theoretical issues, while I imagined real lawyers cutting deals like one salesman does with another. The only course I found of any real significance was criminal law, in which I did quite well.

I found myself lumbering through the classes without much interest. I began to ask myself whether this was where I was supposed to be. After all, if I didn't even like the premise of law school, what could I expect from the legal arena? My feelings about my fellow students didn't do much to sway my developing doubts. I found the majority's motivation so focused on finishing school to enjoy the good life and make a lot of money that I managed to make only a few friends.

I began to feel as if I didn't fit in at all with the law school environment, and I didn't like what this spelled in terms of my future in the profession. I felt isolated and uneasy, so much so that I would comment, that I was more at home on the prison yard than at the school. I was very disappointed with the process and also with myself as I struggled with my motives and direction. It had taken a lot to get to this point, and I had now hit a large snag in the line of my educational sights.

Out of my frustration, I began to search for other types of educational programs that could better feed my political, economic and social policy interests. As luck would have it, I found such an opportunity on the state university campus in Sacramento, in the masters of social work program. It would be within the context of that program that I would become more settled with myself, where my analysis about living in America would be sharpened and where I would find myself presented with a surprising opportunity that would eventually turn into a career.

There were several reasons why I was drawn to the MSW program. I had realized through law school that I needed a process that took me closer to, not further away from, the political, economic and social issues I had become so concerned with. Certainly this social work program lent itself to that. I could become immersed in reading and writing about issues that most concerned me, and become a counselor and advocate for those in the problematic situations I hoped to impact. But, another important reason for my joining the program was that the department's faculty included an individual whose writings I had actually read while in prison. To me, this presented a chance to study with someone who was considered a scholar in terms of analyzing America from a Marxist perspective.

Professor P. was a rather famous individual in the social justice arena and I was quite surprised to find him on the school's staff. He had been teaching at Berkeley's School of Criminology until it was shut down, apparently for becoming too radical, and he found his way into teaching at California State University. I thought that the school was indeed fortunate to have such an intellect. His presence, and particularly what I might learn from him, heightened my interest in the MSW program.

I shifted my academic focus from law school to the social work program, and began to work at developing a career in the social service arena. Without question I was much happier. The MSW program offered the opportunity to study the history of our social policy developments, how these policies translated into social service administrative strategies and how these strategies related to direct service, community work. It also provided, through internships, the chance for students to work in agencies where social work was actually practiced. This too allowed for the opportunity to examine social policy, as seeing what was happening in the community could be compared with what was being discussed in the classroom.

My being more comfortable in this environment did not mean that my frustrations with the academic process had passed. Frustrations continued primarily because most of what I was learning, except from Prof. P., was framed within the democracy-free enterprise paradigm. This meant, then, that the policy issues and administrative strategies that we discussed were based on either liberal or conservative viewpoints, and the direct service issues we worked at stayed primarily within the parameters of those viewpoints.

I was perplexed by the oddity of this circumstance, particularly in a social work program. At a very basic level, I questioned how we could address inequality, an important concern for all in the program, without referencing the limited opportunities available in a highly competitive, profit-oriented, capitalist system. Or, how we could address problems like the changes in the family unit, particularly the mounting stresses on that unit, without couching those changes within the context of capitalism. Simply put, I found it very hard to believe that as valuable as Marx's ideas on America were, they received what seemed to me only cursory attention.

This, of course, I should have expected. I was quite familiar with the highly critical nature of Marxism as well as with what Marx himself had discussed in terms of the difficulties inherent in developing educational processes that were critical of the system itself. But, as was my way, it took the experience of actually being in a program of this nature to make the point clear. And it did impress upon me the thought of how little most people, even at this level, integrated into their discussions and work this important information relative to social problems.

As I passed through the program I continually took notice of this circumstance. I struggled with the lack of dialogue that was apparent, but I used my classroom opportunities to compare and contrast my ideas with those of others. At every opportunity, I wrote about what I was thinking, often juxtaposing liberal, conservative and radical policies in terms of past and present America, and I would then talk about my thoughts within the classroom as much as possible. In these instances I would always try to balance my thoughts with what I had experienced, suggesting that it was the logic of how well the Marxist analysis fit with those experiences, more than anything else, that made it so significant to me.

Many of the professors were supportive of my work, although they themselves didn't produce work of this nature. They encouraged me to continue with my critically analytical approach. They would often comment that, given my background and my continuing focus on both the theoretical and practical sides of ideas, I was someone who might really make a difference in the social service field.

Others however, thought that my radical viewpoint took me too far from problem solving, that the kind of changes I was advocating for simply could not happen within the context of American tradition. For them, my efforts and energy could be better spent and I could get more accomplished if I learned to involve myself more with the system rather than fighting against it. I took their position very seriously as I realized the difficulties implicit in the radical position. I tried to challenge my own views, to alter my course of thinking, but I couldn't accept another course of action given what I had experienced. So, despite the difficulties, I decided to continue on course with what made most sense to me.

In some ways, my radical position cost me opportunities. In one instance I was asked to be member on the committee to revise California's jail standards. Many important state administrators were on the committee, as well as influential representatives from the criminal justice, legislative and other public service arenas. The meetings, which were to run over a three-month period, were considered important, and my inclusion on the committee was definitely an opportunity to increase my potential for future activity. In other words, if I played my cards right, good things could happen.

However, I found many of the members, their proposals, and especially the comments about inmates, rather offensive. When I spoke out about my feelings, which also included rather well-put thoughts on issues of inequality and opportunity, it made the others, even the state official who had invited me, uncomfortable. I guessed that they were expecting some type of token ex-convict, and got something of another sort. Needless to say, this did not serve to enhance the potential of future invitations.

As might be expected, Professor P. was very helpful in terms of my continued interest in the Marxist philosophy. He provided me with a good number of insightful readings and he also shared his experiences from his work at Berkeley. Interestingly, however, we did not really get along. Although we agreed over the importance of the Marxist analysis and how social work, both in theory and practice, didn't reflect that importance, we, almost from the very beginning, didn't agree on where a Marxist analysis should lead one. He was a member of the Democratic Workers party and he believed that it was only through that party and organized efforts of that sort, that large-scale change could occur. For him then, understanding the analysis meant understanding the need for party involvement. But, as I got a bit familiar with the party, I found myself not liking its premise, nor did I particularly like the people involved with the party movement.

On both the party and people level, there was severe criticism of anything American. There seemed to be a need to deconstruct all that was part of the American process. In a strange way, this made me want to defend, at least to some extent, what we did. I couldn't put my finger on exactly what I thought would unfold, but my vision of a Marxist-influenced America was not the same as that of the party's. I was coming to believe that whatever was done on the radical front in America would be done differently than what had been done in other parts of the world. It would be unique, and it would be done with reference to all the good things we had been able to accomplish. Somehow, America would have to embrace itself while it was being significantly criticized.

My thoughts seemed to represent too much of an ideal for the party, and even Marx said that such an approach, what he termed "critical utopian socialism," was misguided. One couldn't hope to make the changes that needed to be made, to overthrow the ruling powers, by including them in a movement for that change. For the party, as for Marx, it was a simple impossibility. So it seemed I was a utopian amongst the utopians. I realized that I was putting myself in a difficult position, but I felt what I felt. Moreover, I didn't like the implication of violence in their thoughts of change. Although I couldn't ascertain their exact views on this possibility, I had a fairly good understanding of violence, and this was not a direction I thought worth going. Consequently, not liking the tenor of the party, or the attitudes of the people in it, I couldn't, in good conscience, follow what they were doing. It was a dilemma no doubt, one I knew would be among many, and one I could not easily dismiss.

Despite my differences with Professor P. and the party, I was often, because of my Marxist perspective, lumped into the category of being a communist, and even accused of being unpatriotic. I found this hard to digest for several reasons. First, I saw my concerns clearly tied to the welfare of our American experiment. And, I was always quick to point out that my position was connected to the evolution of ideas and not the revolution of the masses. The ideas that the Marxist perspective exposed were not, in my eyes, to be used to destroy America, but to make America better. This, I believed, was not being a communist, nor was it at all unpatriotic. Secondly, most of the accusations came from people who had little grasp of the Marxist perspective, except that it related to the Soviet Union. Their mostly unfounded remarks made me think that they were more interested in hysteria than history. Moreover, some of these same people, especially those in the political arena, had agendas that spoke more to their own careers than to concerns about the welfare of America. They were the ones, I thought, who should be confronted with the question of patriotism.

As I passed through the two years of the social work program, I was exposed to a great deal of "thinking and doing" experiences. But, what turned out to be a most significant part of these experiences developed from a suggestion made by one of my professors. In my final term of the program, the Academy of Criminal Justice Sciences called for papers to be submitted for its annual meeting to be held that spring in Chicago. It was suggested that I submit an entry for consideration.

I submitted a paper titled "The Politics of Crime and Criminal Justice-Advocating for an Economic Approach." In a nutshell, it was a review of liberal, conservative and radical views in terms of their respective logic about why crime happens in the U.S. and how we might go about decreasing its occurrence. My overall plan was to clarify each view and its respective ramifications, with the idea that the radical perspective (the economic approach) would make the most sense, that is, be the most logical. About a month after submission I was notified that my paper had been accepted, and it was with a great deal of anticipation that I awaited the opportunity to address a group of the Academy's stature.

The meeting was held over a three-day period at Chicago's Palmer House. There were many sessions planned, and I was to be on a panel with several other individuals who were also going to discuss ideas relative to crime policy in the U.S. Our session was held on the second day of the meeting and, at its end, I was disappointed. It appeared that those in attendance found my presentation interesting, yet I got the impression that few took it with any degree of seriousness. It seemed that Marxist dialogue represented a good conversation piece, but had little value in terms of any actual policy considerations.

I was certainly familiar with this attitude, but I had expected something different from this gathering. I mean, wasn't it fair to presume that at a meeting of this nature, a meeting primarily of ideas, that issues like this would be treated with significance? Shouldn't, in fact, others be discussing similar ideas? Given the dismal state of the criminal justice system, and the failure of both rehabilitative/liberal and punitive/conservative measures to effectively address crime, wouldn't consideration of alternative thought be welcomed more enthusiastically? Was I that far off with my thoughts about the system or how valuable the logic of Marxism could be? Did I make a wrong turn somewhere?

As I listened to other sessions and discussed issues with others, and as I attended the social gatherings or just walked about, I had mixed feelings of naivete and anger. Save a few keynote presentations where everyone was wanting to be seen, and the occasional exchange of business cards with the promise to be in touch, nothing was really happening. People seemed uninterested in getting too serious about the issues. It was as if they had been over them before and already knew that very little would happen as a result of their input. I realized that this was my first time at one of these meetings. Perhaps I was making a premature judgement. But, in recognizing the cynicism and complacency, I had to scratch my head in confusion as to why people would go to such lengths (and expense) to hold a convention like this, with such insignificant results.

However, two things happened in Chicago that really made my trip worthwhile, perhaps pointing to the merits of these type meetings. The first was that I got to see my old friend, Father Barry. We had remained in contact over the three years since I had left Nevada, and I knew he was in Chicago completing his doctorate in theology at the city's university.

Over our five-hour dinner, we covered a great many thoughts about both religion and crime. We talked about how the tenets of Christianity were losing their hold in America, and how he was struggling with this fact as his religion was making adjustments to keep its believers in the fold. For him, the loss of people's faith and their growing cynicism was directly tied to the Church's inability to better define God outside the realm of profit and power, a realm with which the Church had become so intricately tied. He believed that the catechism of his Church could not be effectively reinvigorated until the issues of faith and the tenets of capitalism were somehow untangled.

I found his dilemma very powerful. Even though I had regularly and with deep sincerity prayed for help as my prison troubles began, I had doubts about the current state of organized religion. And, as important, Father Barry's integration of capitalism into his struggles was very similar to what had occurred with my own concerns over crime and other social problems. The criminal justice system and the Church had, at least for us, shared problems.

As Father Barry's train departed that night, I remember feeling a bit afraid, almost shuddering over the sensation. We had both chosen paths, or perhaps they had chosen us, that assured struggling times ahead. I wondered if either of us really wanted it to be this way.

The second thing that happened actually ended up altering my career. The chair of the Criminal Justice Department at California State was also at the Academy's meeting and was present at my session. He hadn't the time at that moment to talk with me, but found the presentation very provocative. He wanted to compliment me accordingly, and to introduce me to someone whom he thought I should meet. Over a cup of coffee I was introduced to the dean of the School of Criminal Justice at the Rockefeller College of Public Affairs and Public Policy in Albany, N.Y. As we chatted, the conversation moved from my past experiences and my presentation to what I might do in the future. The dean wanted to know if I would like to attend his school as a doctoral student, suggesting that a Ph.D. would be of benefit to anything I chose to pursue. He extended a three-year open acceptance, indicating that I had only to let him know a term in advance when I would be coming.

I was very flattered by the offer. In fact, I saw it as the most important part of my Chicago trip. I was excited that someone of the dean's caliber thought enough of me to make such an offer. In contrast to the self-doubt raised over the last several days, the offer buoyed my spirits, providing a form of validation of what I had been doing and thinking over the past few years. It seemed that, just when I was about to give up on my sense of direction, something would occur that would keep me going. Fate, God, luck, whatever...the dean's offer was another example of this fact.

But, this was only half of the second thing. When I returned to California, the chair who had introduced me to the dean asked me

to come to his office for a chat. He then offered me the chance to do
something I had never done before, nor even considered. He asked
me if I would like to teach in his department. He told me that he
believed I had the requisite skills to be successful as a teacher, and
that I would be a welcome addition to his faculty. He suggested that
I think about the possibility, and that he would be in contact with me
about it sometime in the summer months ahead.

It was another flattering offer, one I simply never expected. I
left the chair's office trying to steady my excitement. I didn't know
much about teaching, although I had my opinions about what made
an effective teacher. And, I would certainly welcome, in fact be
enormously proud of, the opportunity to teach at a university. But,
there were some problems. I had to let the chair know that I was still
on parole and probation, and that I would be for another year. Perhaps
in the administrative chain of events, this could not be overcome.
(My parole status was a mini-story in itself, as the judge who originally
sentenced me unexpectedly refused, even given my success and without
any explanation, to release me from parole and probation obligations.
It was unusual, but I wasn't released from these obligations until my
full term, a little over five years, was finished.)

I realized it would require some effort for the chair and the
school to go out on a limb to this extent. Simply considering the
consequences of having a problem develop concerning a faculty
member on parole and probation—an ex-con of the heroin dealer
type—would be enough to derail the idea. I decided to put the thought
of teaching on the back burner, as I had other more immediate
concerns to attend to. I was about to graduate, and I had to complete
my thesis in order to make that happen. I also had my other work and
job-related activities to attend to.

The completion of my thesis was obviously my primary
concern. It was a study on the transition of California's correctional
philosophy from a rehabilitative to a punitive perspective and so it
reflected my interest in the comparison of liberal and conservative
politics. I had worked very hard toward its completion and although
it suffered from methodological problems (in its use of open-ended
questions to support the assumptions in the study) it did provide
insight into how we generally respond to crime in America and where

the shortcomings of these typical responses might lie. A most interesting result of my study was that I was able to provide support for the conclusion that the criminal justice system would be more aptly referred to as the criminal response system, as justice seemed so far out of reach for everyone involved.

My work outside of the university also provided opportunity for thought. During my last year of school I became the criminal and immigration law coordinator for the Immigration Law Clinic in Sacramento. Located in an old church school building along with a food closet, a crisis center, an adult education program and a day care center, and directed by the daughter-in-law of Caesar Chavez, the clinic served clients who were attempting to become citizens, trying to obtain green cards or attempting to legitimize their stay in the country by filing for political asylum. It was my job to help out in all these areas, mainly to prepare and sometimes argue the cases in Federal Immigration Court, but I specialized in those situations where individuals had come to the attention of immigration officials through being charged with a crime. These people faced both criminal sanction and deportation.

I enjoyed the work immensely, especially the people involved with it. Community work, despite the dismal pay, can be very inspiring and this was certainly the case at our clinic. However, a significant number of cases failed, with the most disturbing cases being those where the clients needed more attention than we or they could afford. My experiences at the clinic never let me forget that at the larger, macro level of business and politics, a great deal of work needed to be done.

I also worked with the Seven Step Foundation, a Sacramento group attempting to address the problems of the ex-offender population. In many ways it was similar to the Nexus and CETA projects I worked on in Nevada. It was also designed to help individuals with job development, education programs and personal counseling. I served as a part-time counselor helping individuals with their immediate problems, and also as a board member, attempting to persuade community members to support the program with money and other resources.

We did the best we could at the Foundation, but as with the Nevada projects, the problems of the ex-offender population, given their close correlation to larger issues like poverty and inequality, made the direct service work difficult. Through my work there, however, I was connected to the Prisoners' Union, a San Francisco-based organization attempting to address the larger political and economic issues that were part of the offender to ex-offender problem. I looked forward to involving myself with this organization, and it appeared that through it I might get at those larger issues that so much concerned me.

The Prisoners' Union was a Jesuit organization with a radical taint, bearing a resemblance to Father Barry. Its members were primarily concerned with prisoners' rights, particularly with how the new, conservative-oriented initiatives would affect those rights. Their concern focused on issues like how longer prison terms would affect overcrowding, double and triple celling, less access to prison programs and less concern over inmate legal assistance and medical attention.

But, they also had an eye pointed toward changing the system. The idea was that as attention to prisoners' rights grew, they could be tied to the larger issues, like equality, opportunity and justice, and the possibility of a large-scale movement could be created. There was, in fact, a belief that if prisoners in California could be mobilized, then prisoners, who do most of the work in prisons, could actually go on strike if certain rights weren't adequately addressed. This would then draw a great deal of attention to the problems and perhaps, at that point, discussions over the complexity of prison issues could be developed.

Although there were a number of people in the criminal justice system who supported the union's purpose, the possibility of effectuating this circumstance put most at odds with it. The thought of allowing inmates to wield such power was threatening to these people. In this sense, the union had the potential to raise important issues, even highlight the conflicting attitudes that existed, and so I was very interested in its activities.

My contribution to the union involved helping to review legislation being passed which affected prisoners, and to consider the legal issues that extended from that legislation. At the beginning I liked what I was doing. I was able to use some of what I had learned about the law as well as what I knew about being a prisoner, applying both to the larger issues that concerned me. But, my enthusiasm began to wane as my experiences with the union continued.

I could see that the union, facing so much criticism and controversy, was becoming more concerned with keeping the organization afloat than with the rights of prisoners and the larger issues. This prompted it to spend an enormous amount of time bending or conceding on issues simply out of a need to survive. Therefore, much of the work that I was involved with became secondary to, or at times in the way of, the "politicking" that was occurring on behalf of the organization. I could see that the union was in a difficult position, but I also recognized that it was becoming so co-opted by the system that its strength to actually challenge that system was dissipating.

For me, it was becoming an organization with only token power, and I didn't like being a part of that kind of process. I was frustrated and angry with what was happening, but there seemed little I could do. Although I remained in contact with some of the people in the union, I decided to withdraw from the organization's activities.

The "catch 22" situation of the union was a familiar one. How could you fight to change the system, especially to the degree that it needed to be changed, and avoid becoming part of it? It seemed you needed the latter to do the former, but that in itself seemed impossible. I never liked the compromise that resulted from this circumstance. It made me re-think my ideas about joining the Communist Party, about the possibility of violence and even the concept of revolution. Maybe the answer was indeed there. I also considered, very alarmingly I might add, how much easier, at least in terms of this struggle, a life of crime could be.

In trying to deal with my frustrations, particularly over what I might do with my energy and efforts, I realized again that no matter what might develop in my life, staying involved with education would be important for me. Considering where I started, I had already learned a great deal by holding to this thought, and I saw no reason to change. But, my work at the school was coming to a close. Given my background, I now had the credentials to work at several jobs, but I wasn't overly convinced of their potential. I had the chance to remain in education, to become involved as a teacher at the university, something I felt I could do and something I would surely learn more from. However, that possibility seemed a long shot.

In the summer of 1984, I received an appointment letter from the Criminal Justice Department at California State University. It was only for part-time work, but I was given the opportunity to become a faculty member at a well-respected school.

The chair had indeed gone out on a limb for me. He had taken a sincere interest in my future, and once again I could sense that fortune was smiling down on me. And, almost like a bolt of lightning, I also saw that with my faculty standing I could become more involved with community projects. This, in fact, would be the ultimate realization of the "foot in each camp idea" that I first connected to while in prison. Perhaps it was from this position, particularly with the support of a university, that I might be able to address the issues I was convinced needed to be addressed. I was a bit cautious with my excitement. I knew that there were struggles ahead. Teaching itself was something I had never done before, and I was beginning at the university level no less! But it was with a great deal of enthusiasm, and head-shaking relief as well, that I awaited the beginning of the coming school year.

Chapter 7

CAREER DEVELOPMENT

The appointment letter provided me with a chance for reflection. I was an ex-heroin dealer/ex-con, a person who spent most of his adult life in and around crime. However, I had made a successful transition into the legitimate world. I was now well educated, both in an academic and practical sense, and I had been able to consider a wide variety of issues in the process. I was also a radical thinker, in that I understood the Marxist analysis of capitalism as being significant in terms of how we live and work in America. As I thought about these things, my hope was that I could carry them all into the classroom, providing students with enough information so they could think logically and clearly about the issues presented to them.

My first course was titled "Introduction to Criminal Justice," and it was designed mostly for freshmen and sophomore students who wished to get a general understanding of the criminal justice field. As I was in my freshman term as well, I was happy that my initial teaching encounter was of this nature. I was nervous as I walked into the classroom. I began to write a few introductory notes on the blackboard, and I sensed the students waiting anxiously at my back.

In that moment I was hit by an unexpected wave of emotion. The realization of what I was doing—putting words on a blackboard, in front of college students, in "my" classroom—came over me. I turned to the class and decided to tell them exactly what I was feeling. Here I was, an ex-drug dealer, an ex-con, a wise guy, who never expected to be doing something like this. Man, this was really a trip. If only the boys could see me now!

I could see that the introduction surprised most of the students as much as it surprised me. They were obviously not expecting anything like this to happen. But, I could sense that, even with their surprise, they were put at ease by my openness and stimulated by what they heard. I filled them in on more of my history, letting them know how I had gotten to their classroom. I stressed how important education was in regard to my life, relating the idea that it should have the same significance to them. When I finished my brief review, the students, still a bit surprised by all this, began to ask some very poignant questions about my experiences. I felt energized by our exchange.

So the learning process began, for them and for me. The 55 minutes of class time went by in what seemed only 10. When the class was over the students expressed how much they enjoyed our first meeting and how enthusiastic they were to continue with the course. I was delighted. Although I knew that I hadn't planned things to go as they did, I felt that I was on to something. On the very first day, I liked what I was doing.

As might be expected, the first few terms were a struggle. Although my classes ended on a positive note and the large majority of students provided excellent evaluations of my classes, I knew I was not getting at the issues as well as I had hoped. I was teaching mostly lower-level courses and the material that needed to be covered was covered. But, the political/economic thoughts, the ideas about government, about liberal and conservative politics and about Marxism that I wanted to discuss were, in my eyes, not properly clarified.

I knew this was, in part, my own doing. I was attempting to reference a great number of variables in my courses, and I wasn't as clear as I should have been on how to do it. Couching the material in class within political and economic concerns, especially in explaining the liberal, conservative and radical positions, was not an easy task, and confusion did occur. In addition to this difficulty, I also knew that my strong Marxist influence was bending information more than I liked. My objective wasn't to create a classroom where everyone ended up thinking as I did, but ended up with an interest in thinking. In both these areas then, I had work to do.

But, I could also see that the idea of connecting issues and concerns to more grand political considerations was not something everyone at the university was doing, particularly with freshmen and sophomores. Nor, did the students seem to have secondary educational histories from which this connection could flow. Simply put, a dialogue had not been developed that referenced the material I was addressing. This, of course, made my classes that much more interesting for students, as the information being presented was often new to them. My class was often the first or only one of its kind for many of them. But, having to develop a dialogue about concerns so significantly important was disconcerting for me to recognize.

It wasn't as if I hadn't considered this problem before. Marx himself had talked about this tilt in education, and Prof. P., among others, had warned me about it. I had also felt it in my own academic and community work experiences. But, in my "seeing is believing" way, it wasn't until this point, where I felt I had some direct responsibility, that the situation was squarely in my sight.

We seemed to be developing in America a strong focus on understanding and managing technology, particularly as it related to profit, without the requisite attention being paid to how we could understand and manage each other. This meant that even at the university level, students were ill-prepared to understand concepts related to something as important as how they were being governed. How could people understand what was going on in their country and in their lives without this understanding? Moreover, where, if it wasn't occurring in the educational arena, would this type of education happen? I speculated even further. What did this say about those already working at social problems? Were they taught about all the variables that related to the problems? Did the teachers who taught them know about the variables? Could those teachers know given what they themselves didn't learn?

Again, these doubts had been with me for some time. But, it really wasn't until the end of my second year of teaching, with my teaching responsibilities growing, my understanding of the institution of education expanding and my continual polling of students and teachers alike, that they became frustratingly significant. As this happened, I became more angered with what they suggested. We were continuing to work at social problems while being educated about only some of the variables that contributed to their existence. We seemed destined to fail. In short, Americans were disconnected from America, and as consequential as this appeared, we, particularly with education, were not, and perhaps could not be, addressing this convoluted circumstance. This disconnectedness, which could be termed a form of social alienation, related to the idea that the American people seemed to be unsure of or didn't know what was happening as they looked around themselves. Especially in terms of social problems, they weren't satisfied with much of what they saw. But, particularly given the ideals of America, they were uncertain of how to interpret it, let alone fix it. The result was that people, out of confusion or the misrepresentation that occurred, isolated themselves from the political world, or, for the same reasons, attached themselves to political gestures that were more spin than substance.

Eventually I organized what I considered to be an acceptable design for reaching the points I felt I needed to cover in my classes. From this design I could discuss almost all areas of criminal justice and the other social problems related to it within the context of liberal, conservative and radical politics, in a manner that was simple, clear and concise. I would still get frustrated and, at times, angry over how poorly prepared students were in terms of analyzing social issues. I also didn't like the idea that when they left my class there was little chance for them to engage in further dialogue on the interface of politics, economics and everyday American life. There were others who were doing what I was doing, a scattered few, but I felt I was at least doing my part. And, I was enjoying the opportunity to teach. I knew that the students were thinking more clearly about the American system, and for the time being, this was satisfying enough to keep me at my work.

As I had hoped, my work as a faculty member at the school was accompanied by a continued involvement with community projects. And, as this involvement kept me in contact with the practical aspect of social problems, I continued to learn a great deal about the social service field. In turn, I was able to share what I was learning with my students.

Although I became involved in many projects that exposed me to community and university politics, including the development of the county's dispute resolution center and the university's athletic drug prevention program, it was in developing education programs for the offender and ex-offender population that I became most interested. This was obviously a perfect fit in terms of what I was now doing and had done, so I focused most of my efforts toward these ends. And these efforts presented some interesting results.

My direct involvement with the offender-to-education issue came through an organization situated on the university campus. The organization was a loosely knit group of students, faculty and ex-cons who were interested in all the issues relating to the plight of the offender population. I was drawn to the group by our obvious mutual concerns, and it wasn't long before I found myself arguing in favor of the prison/education issue to legislative committees. There was a bill being proposed that would eliminate funds supporting several important education programs within the California prison system, and I, along with the organization's director, presented the argument that this shouldn't happen. Through a series of events, we eventually were able to persuade the committee responsible for the bill's passage not to eliminate the funds. This of course was just what we had hoped. For me this involvement with the legislative process triggered my interest in education and prison policy even more. In presenting myself as a university faculty member who had actually been educated in prison and who had achieved success, I could make a difference, and I had. I wanted to continue to have a similar impact.

Had I been, at this juncture, more political with my work or more concerned with what others might want to hear rather than what I wanted to say, things might have been different. I had made a small foothold by handling myself well in the legislative process, and I knew I had caught the attention of a least a few members. But I couldn't help myself. As always, whenever I was presented with an opportunity to participate in further proceedings, whether to comment on prison policy or the development of prison programs, I would tie my conversation to the bigger picture. Without attention to that level, particularly a consideration of a critical analysis of capitalism, changes in prison policies would have little effect. This position, of course, put me at odds with most of those I came in contact with in the legislature, severely limiting my chances for other opportunities.

I did have several conversations with a new assemblyman from Santa Monica, who had an illustrious history espousing radical views, and who was an example of sorts. He was so disliked by other members in the legislature that he admitted he was not a good person to help develop any new programs...particularly those related to the conservatively dominated prison issues. Perhaps his example should have altered my behavior, but it didn't.

While wearing out my welcome in the legislative process, and getting more upset about what I was seeing happen there, my interests began to shift toward the juvenile justice system. The administration in that system had made education a priority, and so, mainly through my affiliation with the university, I was given the chance to help develop new program ideas.

I saw and felt so much through this experience that it is difficult to condense. Although the system was designed to help young people, the issues that it had to confront: dysfunctional families, drug and alcohol abuse, violence, poverty, employment, under-education and so on, were well beyond its reach. Most everyone working in the system had become cynical about the potential of anything good happening with the young people. Even the young offenders saw themselves as little more than prisoners, undesirable cast-offs herded into facilities with no real design or purpose. It was indeed hard to find any bright spots in the process, and as I linked what I saw to my own adult prison experiences, I was sickened over what I was feeling. I would shake my head in bewilderment when people said that we needed to make the juvenile system more like the adult one...what in hell did that mean? This is not to say that there weren't some very dangerous young people in the system, individuals who had demonstrated their ability to commit horrible acts of violence. But, they were clearly the exception, and as hard as it was to recognize through their despicable behavior, even they had terrible experiences in their lives.

I tried to keep a positive outlook. The fact that I was an ex-convict and ex-drug dealer helped me to open communication with the young people. I was able to obtain a secondary teaching credential and I began to create classes in the facilities' schools where students could think about, discuss and write on issues that were relevant to their current circumstance. From this process, I would often recognize particular problems that certain students might be having, which helped me in terms of the counseling I was also becoming involved with. In short, I was doing my best to help.

I was enjoying my role in the system and I felt that the young people appreciated my efforts to help. But, trying to stay focused on just this was difficult for me. I was uncomfortable with my thoughts of the larger picture, the problems in the political and economic realm that I knew were part and parcel of these young people's predicaments. If anyone, I believed I should be the person who could make a difference at that level. Yet, with my past frustrations, I felt I really had nowhere to turn to make anything happen. To make matters more uncomfortable, I also realized that I was teaching my students at the university about grasping all the variables in order to understand and effectuate change, yet I couldn't do this myself. This made me feel like a hypocrite; I did not like the sensation at all.

Even though I was growing uncomfortable, I was distracted from the feeling by what I saw as a more immediate way to help some of the young people I met. After several months of working at the school, I recognized what I perceived as a gap in the school's program. I was working with a good number of young people who I thought had the talent and ability, either in music, art or general academics that, with the right encouragement, could well carry them into post-secondary educational environments. However, no special programs were in place to get these young people motivated in that direction.

So, I set upon developing a program to fill this gap. The format was quite simple. We would first identify, through their work in class, the students who had post-secondary capabilities. We would then provide special classes and counseling sessions to work with these young people. We would stress the intrinsic value of education, not necessarily connecting it to job opportunities, with a focus on motivating them to utilize and develop their abilities to obtain acceptance into college. This would be done in conjunction with the community college and the university in Sacramento, and student interns from each of those campuses would be used in facilitating the classes.

Because many of the juveniles, particularly those from undereducated families, tended to see a college or university campus as a foreign place, their mix with the students, as well as the classes we held on the campuses, was important in overcoming their fears. I thought that if the county could develop a pilot project within their detention facility, its success would provide a model throughout the state, with young people in detention facilities and state juvenile prisons being able to avail themselves of the educational opportunities.

As well received as the idea was, and despite the fact that we had put together a very cost-effective budget, the problem from the very beginning was funding. Money was always tight for social problem projects, always an absurd fact given that we lived in such an affluent and advanced system. But there were also other issues. Some said our low budget made the program seem impracticable to funding sources, and that we should therefore raise it. Inflated budgets, particularly on the administrative end, are the rule, not the exception, despite the fact that they ultimately make the project inefficient.

There was "in squabbling" over which department in the system would actually receive the money and control the project (i.e., enlarge its scope of importance) should we get funded. There were complaints that money shouldn't be given to a new project, but to existing ones that claimed they could provide the same service if they had the money. I marveled at this complaint because there seemed to be many county workers with so little to do that they should have thought of this project before I came along. And, of course, there were those who felt that the idea was good, but the young offenders would simply screw the project up as they had done in the past, making it all a waste of time.

My energy for the project was quickly being sapped by this process. Rather than navigate these waters, I decided to turn to another possibility, one that might eliminate the red tape I was now seeing banded across the education project. Two years prior to this idea, I had established my own non-profit organization called Aliance IV. I had done this while still in graduate school with the thought that I might someday use the non-profit base for a program I could develop. Now, I reasoned, was the perfect time to utilize that base. Rather than be a state-operated project, I could set up one of a more independent nature from which I could obtain funding with limited state involvement. This led me to two distinct funding possibilities, both of which are worth explaining.

In conjunction with my teaching and juvenile offender activities, I had continued to work on criminal justice issues, doing some legal work for inmates and staying active in the American Correctional Association, an organization focused on the continuing problems in America's prison systems. As a result, I remained somewhat active with the California legislative process, particularly the Joint Committee on Prisons, a committee developed to negotiate problems and monitor developments within California's growing prison system. From this involvement I discovered what appeared to be a perfect source for funding the juvenile education program.

The Inmate Welfare Fund had been established in California in the late 1950s to help better inmate life. Generated by a 10 percent surcharge on all items inmates purchased at the prison commissaries, the fund was used to pay for help hired at the commissaries and for a variety of inmate program events such as speakers, concerts, special movies, etc. The total amount of money that could be used for those purposes, however, did not appear to match the money actually generated by the surcharge. In other words, given the length of time that the surcharge had been in effect, the amount of goods that inmates purchase on a weekly basis and the number of inmates in the California system, there should have been a large amount of money in the fund. Upon discovering this, it became my hope to attach to the fund, using some of it to support the educational project. I thought this an ideal fit. Adult inmates could actually be using their money for a valuable program directed at helping to keep younger people from similar fates.

I decided that the best way I could make this connection was by bringing the education idea to the attention of the Joint Committee on Prisons. Some of its members knew I had alternative thoughts on politics, but this time my activities wouldn't be pointed in that direction. Moreover, I had developed a good rapport with the committee's primary legal counsel, and I reasoned it would be through him that I could best address the committee with a proposal.

After several weeks of conversation with this man, who thought the idea quite ingenious, it appeared that although the juvenile offender education project was sound, attaching it to the welfare fund would not be possible. In fact, I couldn't get much more information about the fund other than it did exist and money was indeed in it. I asked how much was in the fund (millions by my conservative estimate) and who was responsible for monitoring it. Assuming the director of prisons was in charge, I asked to talk directly with him. My committee associate gave me a less than adequate response, stumbling over explanations about bureaucratic red tape and the like.

I was very surprised by his reaction and asked him why there appeared to be such confusion. After all, with him being a member of a committee whose purpose was to know and investigate these kinds of things, there shouldn't be a problem. He then gave me his twist on the legislative process. He was what he termed a "legiscrat," a sibling of the more well-known bureaucrat. He had a good job, he knew his way around the legislature, he knew who to push and who not to push and he knew when pushing at all was a good idea. In other words, he had a successful career in the making. He said that most of the people working in the legislature, whether state senators, assemblymen or consultants, were in the same situation, and those who intended to stay around had to figure out when it was a good time to battle over an issue and when it wasn't. For him, the matter of the Inmate Welfare Fund simply wasn't battle worthy.

He said all this with a bent little smile, the type that seemed to be asking me for forgiveness as he talked. As cute as the political mask was, I didn't like what I was hearing. Given my prior experiences with the legislative process, I had suspected that most people operated with this kind of "slipperiness," but I didn't expect it of him. Nonetheless, after a month of writing memos, telephoning and talking, I knew the committee wasn't going to help. I did attempt to explore the issue more deeply on my own, even suggesting to the American Correctional Association that it take the issue of Inmate Welfare Funds across the country to task, but I found very little information and very little help.

I sensed something devious, a scandal perhaps, and I talked to others in the field about the matter. But, I would only get referred back to the Joint Committee on Prisons, so I realized what I was up against. I was angry, and I was again stuck in terms of locating a funding source for the education project.

As alluded to, however, this was not the end of my search for funding possibilities. In fact, the next potential source came as a bit of a surprise to me, and was so different that I hope your attention will hold as I explain.

In the early-to-mid 1980s, an energy was sweeping across California, often categorized under the term "new age" thought. In general, this movement involved metaphysical concepts, astrology, iridology, meditation and the use of crystals and stones, all promising a release from conventional thought through the spiritual investigation of the universe. The ultimate hope of this movement was that the energies created by this process would join with the positive energy already existent in the universe, creating a power that would eventually change the world into a human-oriented, conscientious, caring and loving environment.

My then wife was very much involved with this movement and, particularly with the troubles I seemed to be having with the more conventional world, she was continually encouraging me to pay more attention to the spiritual world's potential. Although I had a very basic understanding of what the ideas meant, I had up until this point not really given them serious thought.

Out of half desperation and half interest—I never disagreed with the idea that greater powers, and not necessarily those cited by traditional religions, existed, nor did I object to bringing positive energies together to make the world a better place—I turned more of an ear to my wife's encouragement. She suggested that I look toward the movement for help. Many of the people she had come to know in the movement voiced the same concerns I did, that the focus on the economic aspects of life were actually damaging our future and a change needed to occur. She also noted that a good many of the individuals in the movement were influential "Hollywood" people who were willing to use their influence and money to support ideas that spoke to change. In other words, their "energy" seemed directed toward my efforts.

The connection of my Marxist underpinnings with the new age spiritualism was clearly avant-garde, even for California standards. But, it was intriguing, and not a completely abstract notion. I remembered that one of Marx's important theoretical concepts, the "dialectics of materialism," was borrowed from Friedrich Hegel, an individual very much interested in the spiritual side of man. Hegel utilized the concept of dialectics, which involved a process of discovery through the clashing of opposing ideas, in discussing man's struggle with understanding God. Marx, having no place in his philosophy for organized religion, modified and adopted the concept in reference to how man would discover the ultimate societal (communist) state. In other words, there existed a relationship, complex as it was, between a critical analysis of capitalism and metaphysical considerations.

I realized, of course, that Marxism had enough trouble being understood without being tied to a new age movement. And certainly the reverse was true. Nonetheless, I was drawn to the idea. It appeared to me, especially after talking with several of my wife's associates, that we did indeed share a mutual concern for changing the way we did business in the U.S. Combining efforts might make sense. Moreover, joining forces would mean a broadening of each other's ideas. I saw their interests lacking the political and economic considerations necessary for a society to reach a spiritual understanding on any level, and they saw my focus on political and economic dimensions as lacking any consideration of man's spirituality. The idea of bringing our criticisms of each other together was indeed intriguing. And importantly, this possibility re-focused my desire to address the larger political and economic issues. Our combination of interests could make this a reality.

It was a grandiose notion no doubt, but I was fascinated with the prospect. Perhaps we could build a program, one with almost complete autonomy, where budgetary concerns or program control would not interfere with the program's goals. With the proper design and adequate funding, our ideas could become reality. I realized there could be problems with the state, that our new ideas might cause them to object and that state licensing regulators could give us a hard time. But, even if this happened, given the power and influence involved in the movement, we could force a debate, bringing the problems in the existing system more into the public light. Perhaps we could effect change this way.

I attended several new age social gatherings to better understand the movement. Although I had some doubts about the openness of their thoughts—they seemed to organize themselves around a catechism of rules and rituals that excluded other ideas in the same way that traditional religions, ones they highly criticized, did—the honesty with which they discussed doing something new impressed me. Simply put, I liked their energy.

To verify the potential of what I was talking about and also to better understand each other, I agreed to have several psychic readings done. Two were by a very famous psychic who was the spiritual consultant to an even more famous Hollywood actress who wrote several books on her new age experiences. The psychic, through clairvoyant powers, analyzed my present and past circumstances without being told what they were or had been, with a relevancy toward what might occur in the future. In each instance, these readings turned out to be positive tests for me, as a power to make something happen with education was clearly demonstrated to the psychic. This, of course, served to validate the ideas I was hoping to advance. (Some people see readings as fortune telling, others as a form of metaphysical science. I'm not sure which is the better analysis, but it was interesting that the psychic could recognize so many things about me without being told.)

Through the various social events, I met several other people who had become part of the movement and who coincidentally had similar interests in changing the way the juvenile justice system operated. After a few meetings with these three individuals, two who worked in supervisory positions in the juvenile justice system and one a recent graduate from my university's criminal justice discipline, we decided we could organize a program that would speak to our interests. We could create something new in the juvenile justice arena that included both spiritual and political/economic concepts in an educational environment. If we could do it right, we believed we could create a program format that could be modeled wherever people desired to address similar change.

We arranged to meet twice a week and at our first meeting we decided our ideas should be formed under the Aliance IV banner. We would base our plans on the development of a wellness center, an alternative to a place like the juvenile detention facility. At this center, new age concepts like astrology, iridology, meditation, the power of stones and crystals, readings and nutritional aids/diets could be used to help juvenile delinquents with their individual growth and personal health.

In the context of using these tools, we would also develop a daily educational curriculum where issues like spiritualism and capitalism would be addressed along with the basics of reading, writing and mathematics. Through developing an understanding of the larger problems that existed in their worlds, problems not really of their making or likely to go away in the near future, like the inequalities in the labor market, education and so on, we believed we could help young people recognize and develop the strength necessary to live more constructive lives. We also believed that they would eventually be able to help others in similar circumstances with that same pursuit. We had some concern about the proselytizing effect of our plan, but we tempered it with the thought that we believed in what we were developing. We understood the shortcomings of the current approaches to helping young people in trouble, and our plan definitely presented a more effective alternative.

In about six months we had a completed proposal. It included a description of what the center would look like, the type of colors, lighting and spacing that would make it more emotionally stabilizing and the type of countryside setting where it should be located. The proposal also included ideas pertinent to the development of a new educational curriculum, including alternate forms of teaching, and the daily routine that would be employed in the center, referencing our concerns over diet, the use of metaphysical tools and physical and mental exercise. It also described how we intended to utilize the university's social work department in researching the value of the concepts and ideas we would use. And, it included a description of the staff we would need, one that would have to possess qualifications consistent with the tenor of our program.

At the proposal's conclusion, we tallied prospective program costs. From staffing to supplies, and even with first-year construction costs, our budget, based on housing 30 young people, was very close to those of existing facilities that clearly did not offer the services we intended. With the proposal finished, we began to arrange meetings with people who could support the center's development.

In visiting the people, including several Hollywood notables who had previously expressed an interest in the program's development, it became apparent that the transition from ideas to reality would be more problematic than originally thought. Although these individuals clearly had the money to support the program, and the program clearly integrated concepts they supported, they seemed hesitant to do what they had suggested they would do. They seemed frightened by the prospect of seeing their words and beliefs actually put into action. Among the other stalling tactics was comment that our research component, particularly in that it spoke to scientific convention, was unnecessary. We saw this component as crucial. Without it we could expect little attention from those interested in the effects of the program, effects we did not doubt.

The delay in moving ahead with the program was unexpected and gave us serious cause to think that the people, despite their previous implications, simply didn't want to go ahead with the project. This situation was amplified as we began to face the state's doubts over our ideas.

As I expected, the state voiced some concerns over what we were intending to do, especially given our spiritual and political ideas. These came as we attempted to locate a county in which to house our new project, a process that required state licensing. The concerns were extremely important because it would be from state agencies that we would receive the young people for our program. If we could not address the state's concerns, then we wouldn't have anyone to work with.

Initially, I had anticipated that we could overcome these problems with the money and influence of the new-agers. And even at a minimum, I had believed we would become involved in some form of public debate that would shed light on the system's current problems. But now, instead of supporting the program, the new-agers saw the difficulties with the state as another reason to withdraw support. It was simply getting too complex, and the potential for conflict seemed to unnerve them.

I should have known better, but their tack surprised me. I thought the new-agers shared the same emotions I did about the issues involved, and that they would use their power accordingly. This was clearly not the case. For all practical purposes this put an end to my hopes of developing the alternative center.

For me, the outcome of our year's effort was consequential. I was certainly not disappointed with what I had learned, or with what I had been exposed to. But, I was fixed on the failure. I had taken risks with my ideas before and felt the naivete and sense of self-ridicule that accompany the "fading hope stage" of risk taking. Yet, this time, perhaps because I had become so wrapped in the possibilities of the program, or perhaps because I was feeling the cumulative affect of my past bouts with rejection, it hit me harder. I was depressed and I knew I had to fight the cynicism I felt building inside.

I stayed involved with the plan to establish an education program for young offenders. After another year and through the dedication of a person in our wellness center group, with some assistance from me and the contacts I had already established, a program got underway that helped some 40 young people get into the post-secondary environment. It was a more conventional program and not nearly as elaborate as we first planned. Yet, there turned out to be some rewards for all the effort. Unfortunately, several years later the program, despite its successes, was cut due to lack of state and county funding.

I was in my third year of teaching and working at community projects (i.e., doing "the straddle"), and despite some success, I was feeling a bit anxious. I knew I was doing a good job in the classroom, and the programs and counseling I was involved with were no doubt helping others. But I simply could not get to the point of addressing the issues that concerned me the most. And, there was that lingering feeling that I was suggesting to my students, encouraging them, that this was what one was supposed to do.

At times, I shared my frustrations with my friend, the chair of the Criminal Justice Department. He understood my feelings and began to encourage me to consider applying my anxieties toward another level of education. He suggested with a Ph.D. my observations and thoughts would be better heard. At a minimum, I would certainly gain more insight regarding the issues that troubled me the most. I mulled over his comments. I was in my final year of the open acceptance for the Ph.D. program in New York, the opportunity that had been extended to me while I was in Chicago a few years back. I could take advantage of that. However, although they weren't as encompassing as I wished, I was involved in several important projects in California. And I did enjoy my teaching responsibilities. I also had to consider that my wife had her work and friends in California.

In January of 1987, during a holiday break, I flew to New York to visit my family and to get a better sense of what a potential move might hold. The School of Criminal Justice was rated as one of the top in the country, certainly a plus. And, it was located in Albany, the state capital, which meant that my California legislative experiences could be put to use. In addition, after years at a distance, I could be closer to my parents. These points meshed with my growing feeling that the chair's advice was on the mark. It might well be through earning a Ph.D. that my frustrations of not getting at the larger issues, of not even satisfactorily contributing to development of a dialogue by which this might happen, could be addressed.

I left for New York with my mind set for a return. It was within five months time, that my wife and I, with some anxieties in tow, left for Albany. As could be expected, another set of notable experiences lay ahead.

Chapter 8

ON TO NEW YORK

I was able to transfer a significant portion of my past academic work to the Ph.D. in criminal justice program. This cut the 60-credit course design to the minimum of 30, which meant that I could complete that part of the program in a fairly short time. The dissertation component, of course, would take years to finish. A requirement of the program was that one year had to be spent as a full-time student. The advice from faculty members was that holding a job during this year-in-residence was not prudent, because the course work was extremely demanding.

This posed a problem for me. I needed employment to support myself, and I wanted to continue to stay active in community work. So, despite the overload caution, I began to look for opportunities when I arrived in Albany. I intended to find a position in a community project during the summer and when the fall semester began I would enroll as a full-time student. I had made up my mind that I could do both.

My job search had its ups and downs. I was overqualified for a few of the positions I applied for, and in some cases my being an ex-felon caused a problem. This is a common problem revolving around telling or not telling prospective employers about your past, which is usually considered a negative. I always opted for the former, especially given what I had done since my criminal days. However, I had the strong sense that my being up-front added to the problem.

   Particularly with criminal justice agencies, and despite my resume, my being an "ex" seemed to scare potential employers who perhaps thought I knew too much about the system. I simply couldn't get work in that field, and I suspected that people were worried I might prompt some uncomfortable situations should I be hired. In essence, they were probably correct. Nevertheless, I was disappointed in not being seen in the light of making the system better. However, I did realize that my rejections were telling me more about the system.

   After almost two months of looking, I was offered a position as the director of a substance abuse project located in a community center in Arbor Hill, the minority section of Albany. My work would be to develop and implement a state-funded program for both the young and adult population in the community focused on the burgeoning drug problem.

   The community had a great many problems—poverty, unemployment, under-education, crime and racial tensions— unfortunately the usual conditions present in lower-income, minority neighborhoods. That these problems existed was difficult enough. That they had existed for such a long time had most of the residents convinced that nothing could actually be done about them. They had seen programs to help come and go; so they possessed more than a fair share of cynicism, another usual condition in neighborhoods like Arbor Hill.

   Neither the board of directors at the community center nor I knew what the outcome of my hiring would be. I was certainly qualified for the work. But I would be involved with predominately minority-related issues and I was, well, white. Consequently, my involvement in the project could easily fuel the community's cynicism. It seemed we both looked at this potential problem and decided that it really wasn't one. I understood the issues, I was excited by the challenge and the board was happy to have someone with my experience. Given this, we reasoned that we could deal with whatever might happen. The board demonstrated their interest in having me work on the project by allowing me time during the day to attend school. If not for this, I would not have been able to complete my required "academic year-in-residency."

My work at the center began with trying to decide exactly how to reach the young people in the community. The original plan was to implement an educational program at the center, since many of the neighborhood youngsters came there after school for recreation programs. I wasn't exactly keen on this idea, because it involved more school-like situations directly after the kids had gotten out of school. Additionally, it didn't appear that we could reach as many kids with this process as we wanted. I decided that an alternative to this approach would be to become directly involved with the public school system. It seemed to me that this way we would reach a great number of kids in an environment that was already designed for educational purposes.

I developed a set of drug-related classes, based on a nationally known substance abuse curriculum. With the help of an intern from the graduate school of social welfare at the university where I had become an adjunct faculty member, we devised a plan. We would bring the classes into two of the elementary schools that serviced the Arbor Hill population. We targeted fourth through sixth grades, some 450 youngsters, and scheduled the classes on an alternate, bimonthly basis. We would teach the classes within the context of health studies, fitting our sessions within those times allocated for health concerns. We would then coordinate the classes with projects at the center, including counseling and parent-related gatherings, creating a well-rounded approach to addressing the community's drug concerns.

The board was delighted with the plan, but there was a major hurdle to overcome. The superintendent of schools, known for his policy of not allowing outside agencies to become involved in his district, had to be persuaded. He would be the one who would provide the entry to the schools.

Our approach was substantially different than what was available at that time in Albany. There were the developing DARE programs that relied on police officers, who were unfortunately not well received in many communities, and a strategy that generally tried to frighten youngsters away from drug use. We were educators and counselors who also had neighborhood-type experiences with drugs (my intern assistant grew up in Spanish Harlem), and we intended to talk with the youngsters about their everyday relationships with drugs and the logic of using them. With this openness, our regular visits and our accessibility at the community center, we felt we could establish the kind of rapport with the young people that was integral to having an impact on the drug problem.

The superintendent was impressed by what we had to offer and opened his schools to our program. He contacted the principals, teachers and health officials who could assist us with integrating our plan into the schools' curriculum and we arranged the details accordingly. By the beginning of the school year, we had a program in place that would be as effective as any other in the state.

As the Arbor Hill plan went into effect, my Ph.D. program at the university began. And, for the most part, it proved to be very interesting. The first year of working and studying was indeed demanding and something I, like my professors, would not recommend. I took courses on the death penalty, including a history of the public policy, legislation and legal interpretations relative to this sanction, and on the deprivation of liberty, including a history of our correctional law policies. I also took courses on violence and anger studied through cultural, political and economic variables, criminal theory, including a history of biological, psychological and sociological theory development, and organizational theory about how organizations, particularly bureaucracies, come to develop and function.

In each instance, I learned a great deal, but none of it was really couched within the context of radical dialogue. It seemed I brought the radical view to the issues we covered, particularly as it played out from my practical experiences. The professors were certainly interested in the scholarship inherent in understanding Marxist theory, but they weren't nearly as interested in discussing how the theory might be actualized in the community. The class sessions then, didn't quite match what I thought might happen.

The remaining portion of my coursework, actually over half of it, was devoted to developing an understanding of research-related concerns. Unfortunately, I found this part of the program both tedious and distracting. We would spend months, first learning the concepts related to methodology and statistical analysis, and then applying what we learned through computer-based studies. The quantification of information, especially the hours of attention devoted to computer work, was not something I had expected nor something I liked. I understood that it was designed to prepare an individual for the life of scholarly, social science work, symbolized by the completion of one's dissertation. But, it turned the Ph.D. into a research degree, which, although a fact of modern academic life, was something I couldn't bring myself to accept. Being interested in human issues, I kept visualizing my use of the computer, i.e., technology, as taking me further from those issues rather than closer to them.

I found myself at odds with research being the major focus of the program. It appeared that the gathering, manipulation and presentation of data, which, although not a rule, could be skewed to make almost any point, was so greatly stressed and so time consuming that it detracted from the essence of becoming an effective teacher. In fact, very little emphasis was placed on how a teacher might function in the classroom even though most of the Ph.D. students were actively teaching in the university's undergraduate program.

Since I had already been teaching for several years, I found the lack of classroom focus wanting on several levels. First, I had seen how poor some teachers were in terms of getting information across to students. They could have benefited from some assistance in this area during their educational, Ph.D. training. Secondly, it didn't seem fair that Ph.D. students would be responsible for teaching other students, who had paid a fair amount of money for their education, without any real training. And, thirdly, since academics spend much of their time developing research skills and getting their highly technical work published ("publish or perish" is the motto), it wasn't likely that they would apply themselves to becoming more effective teachers, especially if they had little training in that area in the first place.

Although I understood that research had its place and there was valuable work done being done, I had doubts as to its import. I had seen a number of research projects whose results never impacted the policies they were meant to explore. In other words, there seemed to be inordinate amounts of money and time spent on projects that had little net value. And, in terms of doing research on the nature of capitalism, something I believed might produce invaluable results, there seemed to be little activity. Funding was almost a moot issue for issues in this area, and even if funds could be obtained, there was a realization that little action could be expected from the results.

On the point of research and the money spent, I proposed to one of my professors, a world class statistician and research methodologist who was a part of a multi-year, multi-million dollar study pertaining to juvenile delinquency, that I would "eye ball" a group of young people in his study. I would chat with them briefly about their pasts, review what information I gathered and then predict their future criminality. He could then, in accordance with the study's elaborate and costly research design, statistically analyze and categorize this same group in terms of future criminality. We would then compare the results to see how close my analysis compared to his. Believing that my predictions would at least be as accurate, with less time and money spent, I suggested that we make this challenge a part of the overall study. He responded, with a smile, that he would be foolish on all counts to take me up on my proposition.

As you might suspect, the impact of my thoughts about social science research, particularly its importance relative to maintaining a job in the professorial world, caused serious doubt for me. I was simply not interested in becoming immersed in that kind of work. And, my sentiments had major implications for completing my Ph.D. Its successful completion would hinge primarily on the effectiveness of gathering, analyzing and discussing data pertinent to my dissertation topic, i.e., a good portion of the next several years would be spent doing research. Yet, I was unconvinced as to the value of doing this. It wasn't going to make me a better teacher. Nor was it going to help with my community work, or with affecting policy in the ways I had hoped. I began to think that there was no point in obtaining a Ph.D. other than saying I had one. And, there appeared to be too much involved in attaining the degree solely for its symbolic nature. I was faced with a bit of a dilemma.

After an exhausting first year and a lighter, but still demanding second year, I completed my Ph.D. coursework, obtaining a master's in criminal justice along the way. I decided at that point that the energy necessary for the completion of my dissertation might be better left for another day. This was actually the point where I began to consider writing a book in lieu of a dissertation, as it seemed to me a more fruitful undertaking. But, my academic struggles took on a secondary nature compared to what developed at the Arbor Hill Community Center.

Our education program got off to a great start. My assistant and I had created a very successful program, using music, videos, the newspaper and television, almost anything that could be related to the drug issue, in developing discussions with the youngsters. They looked forward to our presentations and we became recognizable figures throughout the community, the kids sometimes shouting out to us and waving as we passed by. We also received recognition from the local media, as reporters came into our classrooms to publicize our efforts. And, we began to organize activities at the center, which kept the problems associated with drug concerns in the minds of both the young and adult community members.

After several months a tragic event occurred in the neighborhood that cast even more attention on the center's drug related efforts. One evening there were shootings in Arbor Hill and several local young men were fatally wounded. The tragedy stemmed from a drug deal gone bad. This kind of trouble had happened before, and it wasn't the first time that the community became upset over such an occurrence. But, it seemed that for those who had been part of the community for so long, this new round of violence had pushed them to the limit of their tolerance. The community members were outraged and they turned their anger over to the community center in hopes of seeking a response.

Given that we had established a successful program with the youngsters and that we had been trying to involve community members with drug-related concerns, it wasn't difficult to understand that we should take the lead in organizing some type of community action. My thought was to hold a community forum, a meeting where members of the community could come to together to ascertain what, if anything, they could do to address their concerns. With this in mind, my assistant and I began to organize the forum, making flyers and passing them out through the neighborhood announcing the date and time for the community center meeting. We also made the shootings the topic of our discussions in the school sessions and sent flyers home with the youngsters to alert their parents to the meeting. The day before the forum I attached a large megaphone to the roof of my car and traveled throughout the community announcing the meeting. We repeated this process the day of the meeting. I telephoned the mayor's office, the chief of police and any other dignitaries I could think of to announce the forum. The television and radio stations as well as the newspapers heard about what we were doing and began to telephone my office to report on our efforts. I told them all the same thing, that the community had had their fill of drug and crime problems and that we were holding a meeting to see what could be done. I suggested to the media that they come to see what developed. On the night of the forum, we had a gymnasium full of community members, including the mayor of Albany, the chief of police, local politicians and individuals from church and community organizations. Representatives from the newspapers and the three major TV stations were also in attendance.

In assuming the responsibility to monitor the evening's activities, I needed to keep several things in mind. Arbor Hill had suffered the fate of many inner-city communities. Once a lively, middle-class, urban environment, it had become a lower-income, minority neighborhood as people left the city to move elsewhere. The value of the property had declined, the attention of public services had declined and people had to pretty much fend for themselves. It seems that when property values decline, so does the interest in the value of human beings.

Of course, the community members now gathered at the center were well aware of this history of neglect. Moreover, they had been in these "we're going to change things" situations before. This was a part of their previously mentioned cynical attitude. Although I knew I had little control over how the issues might surface, I was hoping that I could minimize the hostilities that developed while giving the community residents a sense that Arbor Hill was indeed their community and their concerns would not go unheeded.

The night progressed successfully, with people voicing their concerns about both present and past problems and discussing what could be done. Ideas like more education and vocational programs were mentioned, as was the need for more and better job opportunities. Community watch groups were discussed, as well as the building of more police substations and establishment of a community-police board. A good deal of attention was focused on the mayor and chief of police in terms of what they might do to better address the problems and facilitate solutions. And, community members also reminded the city hall delegates that many past promises of action had gone unfulfilled and much of what was being said had been said before.

It appeared that the community felt it had city hall's accountability more squarely in its sights that night, especially with the media attention. This was more than evident by the uncomfortable attitudes shown by the mayor and chief of police. They were clearly upset with their lack of control over the night's proceedings. I found out later that the mayor was very upset that I had told the media he would attend the forum without first confirming it with his office. With the media expecting him to be there, he was more or less forced to show up, a circumstance he did not like, and one he felt I was responsible for.

The mayor and police chief both promised they would devote more time and energy developing plans to assist the community with their problems, and that meetings would be scheduled to further detail what and how changes could be made. The community members were quite satisfied with the outcome of the forum although the cynicism was not going away. And, with ensuing articles in the newspapers and reports on television, we looked forward to being involved with a process that could resolve community problems and address political accountability.

A good deal of attention was focused on the center and our school-based program attracted more of the media's eye. I was asked on several occasions to appear on the evening news to comment on drug-related concerns, and I took the opportunity to make it clear that the mayor's office had an almost impossible task of really doing anything about the drug problem. He simply wasn't attached to any policies that could truly address the issues. Having my doubts about the current drug policies in effect, and also doubting the ability of either republicans or democrats to address the underlying problems related to the drug issue, I felt my comments were reasonable. I punctuated my point by suggesting that the mayor either make the long-overdue changes, or simply make the same concession.

My comments were not taken kindly by the mayor's office. I had put him in a difficult spot. Of course, I could have cared less about the mayor's feelings. In fact, I had become acquainted with a number of younger, politically-motivated people who were interested in ousting their local, nepotism-linked politicians in exchange for individuals who would be more active in voicing the community's concerns. I was supportive of their interests, and not really interested in the spot the mayor was in.

I even began to encourage the center's director to get more involved with the political aspect of community work. I felt that as director of the center and a minority woman from the neighborhood, she could speak to concerns from several levels. But, the more we talked about community politics, the more I could see that we didn't have the same thoughts in mind.

I discovered that the director was a confused hybrid of mostly conservative mixed with some liberal thought. In terms of the former, she believed that most of those in the community who were without work, especially the men, were "lazy asses," who simply did not want to work. She seemed to think that the idea of structurally created disadvantages was more of an excuse than not. In listening to her, it appeared that only women could be victims of economic exploitation. Her idea of addressing social problems was to allow business to take care of them through the creation of more job opportunities.

In terms of the latter, she liked the idea that a liberal government would be more willing to spend money on concepts like the community center, especially in the sense that it helped young people, although she objected to paying so much in taxes. She also liked the idea that a liberal government seemed to be more favorable to women, although she believed that that type government was far too lenient with those who used drugs or broke the law. She believed that if you played your cards right, if you were really politically savvy, you could get from the government, irrespective of the party in power, funding for any number of minority projects. And, much to my chagrin, she objected to my comments about the mayor as she saw them hurting her connections to his office.

This caused me great concern. Here was a person, a minority woman, who was being thrust into the community spotlight, who was expected to be a leader in the community, who was being considered as a possible candidate for political office, yet she was really on shaky ground in terms of effectively addressing minority issues. It was my first, hands-on experience with what I perceived as a mostly conservative approach to minority politics, and I was surprised by it.

The director and I had some heated arguments about politics, economics and even the role of the community center. She had no sense of radical politics, which made the possibility of discussing options and alternatives that might be worth noting virtually impossible. So, despite the success of the school-based program, we began to differ on what should follow in the community. My position, and that of others, was that the mayor was in a vulnerable position of accountability, and with that leverage the community could demand that certain things be done. If the mayor couldn't meet those demands, then he should be forced to explain why. In short, he should let the community and the city know what he couldn't do.

As mentioned, the director did not want the community center to be cast in a confrontational role with the mayor's office, but rather she hoped the center would be supportive of whatever he suggested. She believed this would pay off in terms of political and economic support for the center. I, of course, suggested that this was playing right into the hands of the political machine -the democrats who had been in power in Albany for over 45 years. If the center took her preferred course of action and left the mayor to his own devices, nothing of any real consequence would happen in the community. Things would be as they had always been.

Our bickering continued. She accused me of trying to take over as director, which I really had no interest in doing. I accused her of not understanding what she needed to do, which she countered by saying she certainly knew more than me. It was an interesting situation to say the least.

For her, discrimination, both on gender and race levels, seemed untied, or loosely tied in a way she couldn't articulate, to the system.

For me, along with class struggles, they were intricately connected to the inherent inequalities of capitalism. Looking at us, one might have guessed that we would attach different meanings to what we saw happening around us. The idea of a white man taking the position I took as opposed to a black woman taking her position was, well, interesting.

I began to see that my situation at the center, as well as my future working at any other city-related issue, was tenuous at best. The director wanted to fire me, and the mayor preferred that I leave town. But, with the success of the school program, the board didn't want this to happen. I continued my work until the end of the school year, and then, given the discomfort of the work place, I decided to resign. Interestingly, it wasn't, as both the board and I might have thought, my non-minority status that caused this, but my attachment to minority politics.

I was satisfied with the work I had done, especially since the school program was up and running and youngsters were benefiting from it. I had learned a great deal from my efforts as well, especially in regards to "grass roots" minority politics. I wasn't sure in which direction the community would proceed, but I knew there were several eager young individuals from Arbor Hill who could take the political process to task. It was clearly time for me to move on, and with a bit of sadness, I began to look for another position that would carry me through my final year of school. The center still stands today, though not much has been done for the community. The drug problem is as it was and the director of the center is now an administrator at city hall.

My job search uncovered several opportunities. I found what turned out to be a short-term position at a youth center in a rural area outside of Albany. It was a large vocational and educational complex with residential facilities for both males and females. The center provided lower-income young people from New York City the chance to escape from inner-city life while they took advantage of opportunities that could help with their future success. The rules and regulations of the center were based on the idea that the young people needed a sense of discipline in their lives, so the center had its own small security force. In a general way, it reminded me of a mix between the CETA program in Nevada and the juvenile detention facilities in California.

Although I worked at the center for only a short time, my position as a program director provided an experience I had not formerly had. In the context of my work, I was given the responsibility to draft young people who were attempting to get into the center from two of the city's homeless shelters. I traveled to the shelters in Brooklyn and Harlem and chose 45 individuals from the hundred or so who had applied for residency in the upstate program.

I had been in jail, in prison and in several other places of less than five-star quality, and I quickly saw that the shelters matched well with these environments. They were overcrowded and filled with all types of people who were down on their luck. The environments seemed quite lawless, as people fought for bed space, food and whatever else that would provide them with something that someone else didn't have. Despite the good intentions of those who developed the shelters as well as most of the staff who worked there, they were chaotic places with little chance to attend to health or rehabilitative concerns. No doubt these shelters provided a respite from the cold. Perhaps, that's all that could be expected. But for me, much like the jails, prisons and mental hospitals, they were another place that temporarily warehoused or hid people whose desperate situations were tied to our economic and political policies. To select only a few of the desperate but eager young people from the shelters, leaving the rejected rest to...well, to survive, was not an experience I enjoyed.

My work at the center lasted only several months. Amidst administrative changes that threatened my job and my own uncomfortable feelings about the center's shifting policies, I decided to look for work elsewhere. In doing so, I received an offer to teach at a private college in Troy, N.Y., close to Albany. I also found another position as director of a newly-funded substance abuse program housed at a community college in that same city.

I enjoyed getting back to teaching. I was hired to teach several classes, in both criminal justice and sociology, which provided me the chance to integrate some of the material I had recently been exposed to in my own coursework and in the community. As had been my experience in the past, the students enjoyed the classes as much as I did.

The substance abuse prevention/intervention program was designed to integrate the issues surrounding drug concerns into the student, faculty and administrative processes at the community college. There was also hope that the program could develop into a counseling and information center that could help the city and county in addressing the drug problem. As director of the two-year project, it was my job to facilitate these objectives.

Given my other experiences, I had my doubts about the project's potential for success. I did like that it was funded by a federal grant obtained by health officials at the community college. This indicated to me that the focus of the program, rather than being from a criminal justice perspective, would be more in line with the health-oriented philosophy I had come to support. But, I worried about creating a "symbolic gesture" in terms of not getting the concerns that needed to be addressed clearly into the public eye.

As someone who had been in the drug trade, and then studied our war on drugs and interdiction and control policies, I continued to favor the logic of legalization. However, most people, without even understanding the logic, seemed so frightened of the idea that it was difficult to get it out into the open. And, without doing so, I felt that many of the issues connected to the drug problem, i.e. police corruption, unequal enforcement of the laws, misuse of public funds, etc., would go unattended. Several of our initial projects, including a play about alcoholic families and a youth-to-community forum, were very successful. They helped to draw attention to our program. The attention assisted us significantly in terms of developing our counseling services and activities in the community. However, there were problems occurring which provided doubt about the actual impact of the program, problems that I had seen surface in the athletic drug program I organized in California.

For the most part, the faculty and the administrators were very supportive of the program. However, they saw the attempts to include them directly in the education about the drug problem as somewhat unnecessary. Most of them felt that they already understood the issues and that things were so muddled at the political level that rehashing them would do little good. Furthermore, attempts to bring the concerns raised at the school out into the public and into the political arena were not well received. The college didn't want the public to over-think about the idea that there were drug problems on the campus, and those in the political arena didn't want students involved with what they perceived as "adult" political proceedings. For the college's faculty and administration, and for the community's political process, the project was one for "the kids."

The students on the other hand believed that the faculty, administrators and even the politicians knew little about the realities of the drug problem. It was generally their position that if adults actually understood the problem, then we wouldn't be in the dire situation we were in. The students felt it imperative that the adults be involved in the program's efforts.

I supported the student's position as it raised important considerations. As a country, we clearly weren't doing very well with what was seen as a major societal problem. It didn't appear that we had any answers, nor was it clear that we really understood the questions. Although the community college was only a small part of a much larger picture, it was, nonetheless, a part. If the students couldn't get a sense that their discussions, which they took so seriously, were meaningful, then this would create a disinterest, even a cynicism, about the problem. Whatever was done would seem more symbolic than not. In fact, I felt it might be better to do nothing than to feed into this notion. Many of the young people I had come across already had this disinterest or cynicism. It was, unfortunately, becoming a measure of maturity for them. Clearly they couldn't understand its essence, but once it set in, it set in. And, what we were doing on the adult level, at places like the college, seemed to only fuel this dubious circumstance.

I had seen it happen before and it was happening again. We created some interesting and informative programs, and we established a counseling center. But, as far as giving young people any sense that the drug issue would be more effectively addressed...well, not much was being done. I had hoped this wouldn't be the case, but it clearly was. I raised my concerns at a national drug convention held in Washington D.C. My points were met with great interest at the meeting. Mirroring my past experiences with larger-issue discussions, however, not much followed from the three-day gathering.

With the semi-success of the program, I was again sensing how difficult it was for me to do social work in America. It seemed I was seeing all sides of the issues and finding I couldn't really move. I was, in this sense, boxed-in. No doubt, this stemmed in a large part from my Marxist, radical perspective. I had put myself into a position ripe for a career and lifelong struggle. I thought back to my prison counselor, Terry H., giving me that first book and saying, "You might end up disliking me for this." Yet, what I continued to see and feel told me that I couldn't abandon my beliefs.

I wasn't sure how I should continue. I was feeling a sense of burn-out, a real drain on my person. My feelings ran deep, and I knew more education or more project involvement wouldn't change things. The questions were as clear and as serious as they had ever been. Could I stay with teaching and managing projects knowing what I knew? Could I continue to listen to politicians, policy makers and even media people talk the nonsense they were talking? Could I learn to shrug off my feelings and not take my work or my life so seriously? Could I stay mentally and physically healthy doing this? Could I stay healthy not doing this?

On a spring day, about six months before the grant at the community college was to expire, my secretary pointed out a job announcement to me. It was in an educational trade journal she enjoyed reading, and being used to my grumbling about what I would do with myself, she thought the ad a perfect match me. It was an announcement for a criminal justice teaching position with the University of Maryland's European Program. It promised not only a teaching experience, but the chance to travel and to see Europe. Although I didn't take it seriously at first, it was only after a few hours deliberation that I called the university to inquire about the possibility. Perhaps I needed time away from the American process, to see other places and other processes, to get a sense of how democracy, capitalism and Marxism had been mixed in the "old world."

I had the uncomfortable feeling that I might be running away from things, that I simply couldn't withstand the stresses of the workplace, that I was a quitter. These feelings were more than balanced by my belief that I wasn't really running from anything, but actually moving toward something, something that would help me better understand the questions that surrounded my thoughts. I wasn't a quitter but, in fact, I was actually holding to the ideas that very much concerned me, even though I was getting pushed around in doing so.

Within four weeks of submitting my application for the position, I received a note arranging for an interview at the University of Maryland. I was hired shortly thereafter and in August of 1990, I was on my way to Europe. On the flight over, I recalled where I had been and thought about where I was headed. So much had happened—prison cells, programs, helping people, teaching, learning—and surely there were more experiences on the way.

PART FOUR

Chapter 9

EUROPE

I arrived in Frankfurt, Germany, and a representative from the university met me at the airport. His responsibility was to drive me to Heidelberg, an hour south, to the school's administrative center, and to give me some information about living in Germany. My teaching assignment at least for the first year would be in Deutchland. As we drove I could hardly pay attention to my guide's comments. I looked at the cityside and then the countryside, recalling what images I had about Germany. Uncomfortably so, there were recollections of black boots, goose-stepping, the swastika, "sieg heil," hide because the Nazi's are coming, trains with troops or prisoners, our enemies when we played our kid war games—a distantly strange yet powerful legacy of war and remembrance. None of it seemed possible as I looked at the elegant Frankfurt skyline and the beautiful green hillsides that spread out toward Heidelberg. But, the periodic English road signs, indicating the American military facilities that dotted our route made my childhood images remain close.

Arriving in Heidelberg, however, brought other thoughts to the forefront, particularly of my father's "Student Prince" record and Mario Lanza singing "every day is like a holiday...when its summertime in Heidelberg." The city looked picture-perfect, and as we drove through downtown, I began to really sense that I was in Europe. The streets, the streetcars, the street-lamps, the signs for the castles, the old buildings, the people—this wasn't a city made over to look European, it was Heidelberg.

As we pulled into the administrative center parking lot, I realized how excited I was. I thought about how my good fortune had continued in helping me find this opportunity. I sensed that my struggles and frustrations over what I had experienced stateside would be, if not better understood, at least lessened, as this experience unfolded.

I had a brief introduction, and then I met with several social science faculty over lunch and they filled me in on some of the practicalities of teaching in the program. I also began the required paperwork for obtaining a driver's license and an I.D. card, both processes associated with military operations. While getting everything in order, which took several days, I was housed at a local German hotel, which initiated me to a few of the different customs that would become part of my daily routine.

These differences ranged from what the Germans eat for breakfast to when they open and close their stores. The most difficult difference related to my lack of understanding the language. Although a good number of people understood basic English, I was frustrated that I couldn't really express myself very well. Nor could I understand what was being said around me. I wasn't at all happy with this, but I quickly reminded myself that this was a part of traveling and learning. (Many Europeans speak not only English, but three or four other languages as well. This is, of course, due to their proximity to the other countries as well as their interrelated historical and commercial transactions. When Americans like myself don't know the languages of these countries, it gives the impression we have a certain non-caring attitude. Unfortunately, this fuels an already existing smugness attached to American ethnocentricity.)

I was given my first assignment, which would run for two years, in Ramstein, Germany. Located about an hour west of Heidelberg, this was military headquarters for the airforce stationed in Europe, which meant that the base would have a large education program. I lived in officer's quarters on the base for several weeks while I located a place to live and purchased a car. The university offered some assistance in terms of housing referrals and auto buying, but being left on your own seemed the best way to learn about the area, language and local customs. It was a bit of struggle, but I found both an apartment and a car within a few weeks, and I was then ready to begin my teaching activities. Surprisingly, I found a place that happened to be owned by a German police investigator. This happenst· nce provided for interesting chats between us, and he even helped me to arrange a visit into a German prison to talk with American prisoners being held there.

The University of Maryland Overseas Program itself began in 1949. The school's primary mission was to provide college courses and degree programs to U.S. military personnel and other government workers stationed in Europe and Asia. When I arrived in Germany, the program serviced some 30,000 people in 25 countries and it had extended the courses to the nationals in each respective country. These individuals from the host countries had an affiliation with our government activities that allowed them to participate in the college programs.

There were educational offices at almost every base around offering courses similar to any college curriculum. The classes were most often held in the junior or senior high school buildings on base, although any available location would suffice. Since it was the university's responsibility to provide courses even at the most remote or smallest bases, this meant traveling to those places, and sometimes residing there, as well as holding classes in some non-traditional settings, i.e., barracks, shelters and even on ships. Most classes were held on week-nights, but there were also daytime and weekend courses to accommodate the varying military schedules. The "ad hocness" of some of these circumstances (i.e., making due with what was available) drove the more traditional academics quickly back stateside, but I found myself enjoying the experiences from the very beginning.

I had not had much contact with our military system in the past. Most of my thoughts about it had been formed by books, movies or conversations with others who had been part of it. Of course, growing up in the Vietnam era put a certain spin on its purpose. I had been fortunate enough to avoid the Vietnam experience through the draft lottery, but I was certainly aware of the consequences of that war. This awareness, coupled with my radical view focused on the military as an extension of, and enforcer for, our problematic capitalist system, cast a dubious shadow over a process I was now going to be in close contact with.

The bases were generally designed around the same plan—an American community with food and clothing stores, schools, places of worship, gymnasiums, laundries, gas stations, movie theaters, restaurants and bars, fast food places, ball fields, golf courses, dormitories, houses in neighborhoods and almost anything else that might bring the comforts of home a bit closer. These things usually surrounded the military facilities, where the bulk of everyday work was performed. As would be expected, the larger bases had more of all these details, while the smaller and more remote installations had less. In either case, the surrounding cities or villages offered as much as they could to accommodate the American presence and the availability of American dollars with pizza and burger shops, American style nightclubs, etc. It was common to see American military men with girlfriends or wives from the host country, a circumstance that also seemed related to the offerings of the local areas. (Many variables came to bear on these type relationships, but a significant one, particularly because I had never thought about it before, is the power of American citizenship. Often, an American soldier represents the only opportunity for a foreign person to attach to that power and its implied freedom. It seemed to me that many relationships developed accordingly. Throughout the history of the world, very few societies can lay claim to such a valuable citizenship.)

As a member of the University of Maryland faculty, I was part of the Department of Defense's large entourage that followed the military process. Along with the secondary school personnel, the service providers and government contractors, we were provided with I.D. cards that gave us full membership in the military community. This meant that we could take advantage of all the amenities on the base. So, we were able to live in a foreign country, engaging in its culture and beauty, while still having a certain sense of comfort close at hand. This was something special, and certainly something that people from other countries could not really identify with.

If we chose, we could purchase our food and clothing, as well as cars, insurance, gasoline and almost everything else at minimum cost in base stores. We also had access to all the recreational facilities, restaurants and clubs that would have been very costly to enjoy on the host country's economy. As an avid golfer, this meant being able to play golf at well-appointed military courses for a minimal membership cost, rather than at the very expensive local country clubs. And, through my golfing activities, I became associated with a good number of people, from generals and wing commanders, to foreign and U.S. diplomats, all of whom provided insight on whatever ideas I might be considering. I always had questions about what was happening in Eastern Europe and with the European community, and it was interesting to get the perspectives of those connected to the military regarding my thoughts. I also had the possibility to invite people to the base for golf, dinner or whatever, and this was a good-will gesture that nationals enjoyed very much. These opportunities provided me with the chance to talk with them about my thoughts as well.

For those of us who had not been exposed to the military, there were opportunities to observe the daily activities surrounding its processes, particularly the maintenance of machinery and equipment, as well as the personnel necessary for its missions. As much as I had a distaste for what the military industrial complex represented, I could see the power that it wielded as well as the effort that it took to maintain that power. I simply hadn't considered the military in this context before.

As I became more familiar with people in the military, from privates to generals, I could see that they had enormous pride in being American. I admired this trait. However, most weren't particularly concerned with America's political issues. Their mandate was to prepare for conflict, and discussions on ideological concerns, save those tied to the military budget, didn't seem to capture their interests. This part, particularly given their "enforcer" mission, bothered me. (I recall having several conversations with high-ranking officers as to what direction American ideology was taking. Although these conversations were interesting, what stays in my memory was a comment made by a soon-to-be general. He said that for the most part, ideology was unimportant, that an effective war machine could fight under any ideology. In fact, he remarked, it wasn't ideology that shaped the world, it was the power to enforce it, and that's of course what our military did.)

Being around the bases in foreign countries certainly added credence to his thoughts. It wasn't hard to think that perhaps America couldn't get along without this enormous power. After all, having a strong "arm" was as important as anything in terms of getting along in the neighborhood. Why should getting along in the world be any different? I realized that this thought was in many ways at odds with the ideals of peace and harmony, with a world that so many, including Marx, had hoped would come about. But, perhaps, it just couldn't be that way. Perhaps, we humans were as combative as thinkers like Thomas Hobbes made us out to be, and warfare and strong militaries symbolized this fact. Although I had entertained these ideas in my past educational endeavors, and to some extent lived by them in my criminal days, they had, for the most part, lost their import. Now, within the context of my current experiences, I was reconsidering them in a different light.

Other reconsiderations developed via my teaching experiences. I was primarily responsible for teaching criminal justice courses in the University program, although I would become increasingly involved in the sociology discipline. In my second year in Germany, I was asked to teach a six-credit, two-term course called "Crime and Delinquency Prevention." The course included a large range of concerns related to theory, politics and economics, social policy and direct practice. It was almost like a final review for those finishing their degree in the criminal justice curriculum.

The major text suggested for the course was *Crime and Human Nature*, by James Q. Wilson and Richard Herrnstein. I was familiar with this controversial text—its reference to biological determinates as causal factors for crime had caused quite a stir in the academic community. I was not at all in favor of biological interpretations for behavioral motivation. My academic background had been primarily based in political, economic, and sociological considerations, but I decided to use the text as a base for course discussion. I reasoned that while we critiqued the biological references featured in the book, the sociologically oriented issues that Wilson and Herrnstein relegated to a secondary position of influence would come favorably to light.

Although this is generally what happened when I taught the course, I found myself intrigued by the tenor of the book. The basic ideas put forth could be framed quite simply. Rather than concentrate solely on what the family and environmental circumstances bring to the table in terms of affecting a young person's motivation toward criminal behavior (i.e., the sociological view) we should concentrate, at least in equal part, on what the young child brings to the table. If a child has certain characteristics, like a chemical imbalance, a high tolerance to pain, a dulled sense of emotion or highly impulsive or aggressive traits which are biologically induced, and these characteristics can be shown to contribute to dysfunctional or criminal behavior, then it is within the realm of biology that we must look to prevent or mitigate that behavior.

The authors provided research data that supported these biological considerations—a good portion of the research began long before psychology and sociology came along—and reasons as to why biology hadn't been considered as significant as it should. They noted that biological explanations lost their footing in academia at about the same time we began to see the atrocities resulting from Hitler's use of this logic against the non-Aryans in Europe. Simultaneously, a growing interest in sociological interpretations for referencing behavioral patterns, made the use of biological references less significant. But, as the authors imply, we may have thrown "the baby out with the bathwater," because the possibility that biological factors affect behavior cannot be ignored.

Of course policy implications are dangerous, in both a racial and class sense. For example, suppose one opens the door to any male prison and notes that 50 percent of its population is black and 80 percent of all the males are from the lower class. And, suppose that same person looks at the unemployment rate and notes the high rate of black male unemployment as well as that for all lower-class males. And, suppose that this person looks at the educational arena and notes the high rate of undereducated black and lower-class males. All of these suppositions are proven facts in our society.

In a sociological sense, the reasons for these facts would be referenced by structural arguments, focused on inequality and lack of opportunity. To address the problems we would have to fix the conditions of inequality and opportunity. But, if one takes the biological tact, as Wilson and Herrnstein suggested, it appears that black males, and lower-class males in general, could have some biological deficiencies that led to their problems. To address these biologically-based problems we would have to focus on fixing the conditions within these individuals. This could entail anything from drug therapy, to mental and physical tinkering to stop anti-social behavior, to sterilization and even genocide to prevent people of "this sort" from breeding. Again, Wilson and Herrnstein imply that it was this potential "evilness," particularly as evidenced in Hitler's Germany, that was the primary cause for our shelving biological research in the 1930s.

There were problems with the research methodologies that supported the authors' data and nothing really conclusive could be drawn from any of it. Many academics were also up in arms over the potential misuse of such research, especially in light of its lack of scientific integrity. But, what Wilson and Herrnstein seemed to be saying--that research had been done in the area and more research needed to be done simply because biology had a lot to do with people's behavior--made it difficult for me to dismiss the book's general theme. It was becoming apparent to me that despite my training as a sociologist and my distaste for biological considerations, particularly that certain groups of people are born genetically inferior or superior, biological considerations were indeed important in referencing human behavior. In simple form, I asked myself whether biology wasn't at least fifty percent responsible for what I had done or might do. And, weren't some of the individuals I had come across in my past skewed in the way Wilson and Herrnstein suggested? Was it only social forces that separated people like me from people like my old prison mates Hazen and Jesse B.?

I began to think that like with Marx and the considerations related to capitalism (i.e., isn't what we do in America at least 50 percent tied to our economic/capitalist motivations?), I had not been adequately exposed to the variables, which, in turn, fed into my disbelief about them. It was possible that the tenets of biological determinism were as important to understanding behavior as the tenets of capitalism. If one imagines a biologically-skewed individual in a system that, among other things, tends to turn the "greed key"...well, we will have some dangerous sorts out there.

Of course, I did not want to accept any of this. I didn't like considering these nature-nurture issues in this way. I clearly understood the "Hitleresque" policy implications of biological referencing. Given my criminal past, I myself could have been cornered in this light, and I shuddered at the consequences.

But, could I let the possible mismanagement of the research cloud the value of the research itself? Shouldn't biological concerns be attended to with the same openness that I argued capitalism should? Again, I was uncomfortable with these thoughts, but I couldn't escape them. And, as I continued to teach the course in the years that followed, I decided to raise these points as I had come to see them, with the questions and fears being clearly expressed as part of the class. In all fairness, there was little else I could do. (Interestingly, I was living in Germany as I seriously considered these ideas and Hitler's image was always close in my mind.)

I began to teach more in the sociology discipline, and although the questions about the nature of man didn't diminish, the focus of my classes was on political, economic and social policy concerns. Much of what I discussed revolved around charting our country's development through the 20th century and the transition of America from a depression-ridden country to a World War II victor. I always discussed this transition in terms of what happened in the 1950s— the U.S. rebuilding the world, spreading our ideology and military in the process, with our growing economy, jobs and prosperity, and our belief that America was the "best place in the world." I talked about the civil rights movement and how this brought the ideals of America into question, particularly how the movement pitted the freedoms of white America against the equality concerns of many of its other citizens. I was always a bit upset that so many Americans referenced freedom and equality as if they didn't tug at each other, as if the responsibilities inherent in having an equal society do not mean tempering some individual freedom.

The radical movement was referenced in this period, and the years that followed brought to light a change from liberal to conservative political agenda. Issues like racism, sexism and crime were framed in the context of these years as were the changes in our cities, the workforce, education and the family. The students obtained a good deal of information from this approach and I enjoyed teaching the classes. My having been a part of many of the "historical" concepts we were discussing made things interesting for both of us.

The students in the program, mostly military, were different from my stateside students. They were older; they had families and jobs and were more mature. They were also a bit more conservative in their thinking—a strong variable in their opting for military life— but they were quick to pick up on ideas that seemed logical, even if doing so went against that conservatism.

In a discussion on the American military and its relation to capitalism, I offered the suggestion that given their lifestyle, i.e., their similarities in dress and appearance, their own TV station with no product commercials (all the programming breaks were filled with commercials about how to be a thoughtful parent, or an aware and healthy person), their own schools, their own legal code, the fact that everyone had a job, health benefits, some parity in the pay-scale and so on, that they were very much a socialist organization.

This observation came as quite a surprise to most of them. However, the comparison seemed consistent to them, and rather than upsetting them, they instead found it paradoxical that it was the socialist structure they tend to fight against. I also presented my thoughts to two generals I golfed with, and, without much objection, they agreed to the military-to-socialism comparison, citing that discipline and a focus on mission were better served by these means.

My first two years in Germany and the following two years in Spain and Italy provided a variety of experiences. I lived "on the economy," which meant that I resided in the cities or villages rather than on the military base. Getting used to the local customs, food, language and money exchange was always interesting. It was clear that living in a foreign country was much different than merely visiting.

Individually, the Europeans seemed much like Americans. They worried about their children, families and communities. They were decent and funny, they loved and hated and they hoped the future would bring the best. But, in a collective sense, particularly in terms of their political, economic and social arrangements, they were markedly different from us.

The European systems seemed to reflect an understanding of socialism, capitalism and democracy much more than we did. Taxes were very high in most countries, but they subsidized generous welfare systems, including health and pension plans. There also seemed to be a more realistic focus on job creation for everyone. And workers, no matter in janitorial or corporate uniform, were given respect for the work they performed.

The situations were far from idyllic, however. Problems with high taxes, loss of jobs and stagnant bureaucracies, especially in countries like Spain and Italy, were very evident. But, even in those countries, a sensitivity toward life always seemed present, one that was difficult to detect stateside. Some argued that this notion about life served as cause for the financial decline of European economies— more attention needed to be focused on the practicalities of business. But, the continuing conflict between socialist and capitalist principles evidenced that this belief wasn't shared by all the people. As I traveled and talked with people, especially students, it was interesting to note how well versed they were in understanding the differences of the varied political and economic perspectives.

The University of Maryland operated under an eight-week term system. We had two weeks of free time in between terms, plus a one-month break at Christmas and an additional three months if you didn't work during the summer. There was ample time for travel, and I took advantage of it whenever I could. I visited almost all the European countries, seeing the sights and talking with people as much as possible.

My conversations centered on the Europeans thoughts about America. Our unmatched freedom was something they marveled at, as they did over what they saw as our misunderstanding about the responsibility that freedom demands. As for their thoughts about Europe, they were sensing the growth of troubled times. They voiced concerns that the developing European Union might make Europe more competitive in the world but leave individual countries vying for power. They also worried that the focus on economics would negatively impact social policy. The discussions I had were very interesting, and they helped to frame what I saw as I traveled.

At times it was almost like a dream, as I wandered through the countryside and through the streets of cities like Paris, Rome, London, Amsterdam, Lisbon, Athens, Seville, Brussels, Vienna, Zurich, Munich, Venice, Lubijana and Prague, and through the marketplaces of countries like Morocco and Algiers. These were incredible experiences, and, on occasion, I had to wonder how I had gotten to the point of being able to do what I was doing.

Eastern Europe was developing and travel there added to my experiences. I was in Berlin shortly after the wall's demolition and traveled into the eastern section. I was struck by the clean, 1950s-style city facade that lay on the western border of East Berlin and the poor conditions that existed within minutes of a walk eastward. I tried to talk with people about their experiences as I shopped the open-street markets, but being an American, dealing with people's lingering suspicions about foreigners and not understanding the language presented too many barriers. On the west side of Berlin, it was much easier to find people to converse with.

Those I chatted with were most concerned with how the new Germany was going to be able to take care of its new citizens. I realized that for the first time since WWII, Germany was now going to have a visible, "out in the open," lower class to somehow deal with. It appeared this would have a major impact on the future of their social democratic government, as the more prosperous individuals would be forced to become more responsible for those in the lower class. Perhaps this responsibility was something that wouldn't be so easily accepted. In fact, Italy was facing a similar problem with the prosperous, industrialized North supporting the less-affluent, agricultural South, and this was causing a northern-based secession movement in that country.

I never had the opportunity to travel to Russia, but I did get a chance to meet with Russian people and to talk with them, via translator, about the sweeping changes in their country. On one occasion, I chatted with Russian high school students who were visiting an American school in Germany. We talked about their thoughts about the changes in Russia, and to what extent social problems like crime and drug use would be affected by those changes. The young people were all fearful of the developing lawlessness there, but were excited about the new freedoms, especially the things they could now buy, that were part of the change. I had a similar reaction from Russian postal administrators I met in Paris. My girlfriend was the translator/chaperone for their trip to France to study the French postal process, and I had the chance to go along. The Russians said they were very happy to experience "western freedoms," but they too were unsure of how those freedoms would play out in the hope for creating a well-balanced Russian society.

Given the situations, as well as the possible suspicions over my questions, I wasn't sure what to make of what I was hearing from the students and the postal people. But, taking their comments into consideration, along with what I experienced in Berlin and what was happening across western and eastern Europe, I began to think more about the concept of freedom. It meant so much to the people I encountered, and we Americans were envied for having so much of it. I was convinced, however, that we really had lost sight of what the concept of freedom actually implied.

By a twist of fate, I also found myself involved with a project in Hungary. I had attended a conference in Vienna that focused on the development of the European Union. Having obtained enough information, I found myself with several days remaining on my vacation schedule, as well as travel left on my Eurail pass. Since it was only three hours away, I decided to visit Budapest, a city I had been hoping to see for some time.

I boarded the afternoon train. As I looked for my cabin, I noticed a pretty woman sitting alone in her cabin. After locating my place, and in the best of the "James Bond tradition," I began to study from my Hungarian guide book how to ask her about clean, inexpensive lodging and good places to eat in Budapest. I didn't have a good sense of what I was saying, but I entered her cabin and stumbled through my rehearsed questions anyway. She listened intently to my Hungarian "goulash" and, when I was finished embarrassing myself, asked me politely, and in perfect English, if I spoke English. I felt a bit silly but I was happy to meet a person whom I could talk with.

We talked for the entire three-hour trip. She was from Budapest, working as a translator for a group of Hungarian business people in Vienna. This group was hoping to develop economic contacts for projects being developed in Hungary. I began to ask questions about this development because I knew so little about the status or history of Hungary. She explained that her country, much like the rest of Eastern Europe, was now in a major transition period, moving from the old socialist-ruled structure to a more modern social democratic form of government, with a strong emphasis on developing free-market, capitalist principles. It seemed that Hungary, even under its previous rule, had been allowed to establish an informal, western-style economy. It was by no means up-to-date, but it did give the people a sense of living and working with modern market principles, which gave them an edge over other East European countries in terms of future economic development.

Hungary then was in a good position to attract western investment projects. Despite the edge, many Hungarians were cautious about the advancement of capitalist principles. Relying on the thoughts of Marx, from which their former government had formed, they recognized the opportunities in the offing, but also the risks. These risks, particularly of the growing attention paid to making money over and above the attention paid to human, socially problematic considerations, were of greatest concern.

As we talked, my mind raced. I was seeing the potential to examine this socialist-to-capitalist transition in Hungary, particularly how it might affect social problems. I mentioned my thoughts to my traveling companion, and in trying to explain them more clearly, I began to talk about myself and how my interests over the issues had developed. She found what I had to say most interesting, and more importantly, insisted that I meet her closest friend in Budapest. This friend was an important member of the sociology department at the university in Budapest, and she was also in charge of the family crisis centers located there. Additionally, she wrote for, edited and published a journal that spoke to the concerns over social problems in Hungary and Eastern Europe in a manner that appeared consistent with my interests.

My traveling companion gave me Dr. Kati L.'s. phone number as we arrived at the Kelety station in Budapest. She also gave me the name of a hotel that turned out to be perfect for my purposes. She promised that she would give her friend a call as soon as she arrived home, and suggested that I phone the woman the following morning to arrange a time to talk. I did exactly that and, as luck would have it, we were able to meet late that same afternoon.

I was overwhelmed by what happened at this first meeting. Actually, I was overwhelmed by the entire occurrence. Kati met me at one of the crisis centers she supervised. She was a most engaging person, bright and energetic, and very much concerned with the problems of her country. Her parents had been freedom fighters in Hungary's revolution in 1957. Her upbringing had fueled her sentiments about social problems and political activity that led her to a career as a teacher, writer and director of the family crisis centers.

She showed me around the center, explaining that as ill-staffed and poorly-equipped as it was, it was a place where problems like drug abuse, violence, delinquency and family discord could be addressed. The place seemed clearly out of date, which Kati recognized. Her hope was that things would get better, but her fear was that they might not.

We sat in her office, and over coffee we chatted about the problems in Hungary and in the developing East European world. We were instant friends. We talked about the struggle ahead for the countries that were now trying to enter the economic markets of the world with new political and economic structures. Would investors be willing to chance investments in these unstable environments? Would the people, so used to simple work processes, be able to work in the more modern ways? Would they be able to deal with the stresses of the free market? And, importantly, how would social problems fair under the transition from socialist/communist environments to those more focused on capitalism?

As Kati and I talked, comparing her country's situation with that of others in Europe and with the current situations in the United States, I became convinced that a project could be developed to speak directly to the issues that permeated our conversation. I asked Kati whether she would be interested in developing a project through which we could study and write about what happened with Hungary's transition. I suggested to her that the project would be of value not only to Hungary, but also to other countries attempting a similar transition. In fact, I thought, the information would be valuable to the U.S. as well, as the concerns of capitalism and socialism were something we clearly needed to know more about.

Kati was immediately full of energy about the idea. She speculated that since I was a criminologist, and since the rising crime rate was a growing concern in her country, and since her center had to deal with the stresses and consequences related to crime, we could use the center, most likely with a focus on juvenile delinquency, to develop the project. If we could organize the study properly we would be able to analyze the problems of delinquency within the context of the upcoming political and economic changes. At the same time we would put into motion a project whose political and economic framework could be used to study other social problems.

In other words, once we organized the political and economic variables that concerned us, i.e., those of socialism and capitalism, we could plug in any social problem to analyze how it might be affected by a change in those variables. From this analysis, we could hope to have an impact on social policy and direct service concerns as well. It would take a lot of work, but the idea had tremendous potential. Furthermore, Kati had several colleagues who were already doing work of this nature, but it was not organized in the manner we were considering.

We both felt that we had stumbled across an idea that would allow us to address many of our mutual concerns. The project was connected to what would be unfolding in Hungary, and it could happen by simply watching and documenting what happened there.

In the midst of our excitement and the strange feeling of being able to almost touch what had seemed like an impossible idea, we noticed in unison how late it was. Hours had passed in this, our first meeting. I had another day left in Budapest and I would use it to see as much of the city as I could. Kati had to travel to another city in Hungary as part of her family crisis center responsibilities. As we parted we were sure that what we talked about could be continued through letters, phone conversations, and, hopefully, other meeting times. This turned out to be the case.

Over the next three years, I would make many trips to Budapest. On my third trip, Kati brought together her friends and colleagues who were already working on the political, economic and social problems in a way that was consistent with our interests. We all decided to develop a non-profit, research organization, calling it the Social Research Group. In terms of its not-for-profit status, the SRG would be among the first of its type under the new Hungarian laws, and this in itself made the project's development exciting. And, my having expertise in this area made my introductory contributions to the group more valuable and more acceptable. It is not easy to become involved with social problems in a foreign country, and this seemed especially true being an American. Given our lack of understanding about what transpires in our own country, particularly as it relates to capitalism, people in other countries tend to be skeptical about our understanding of social problems in general. This, along with the exploitive history tied to capitalism, makes them leery of our intentions. In this sense, I had to be very careful.

I had to let people know that I knew about capitalism from a Marxist perspective so that I would be accepted into their working group. But, in doing so, I didn't want to give them the impression that I had a personal vendetta against America, even though I had some problems with what we did. I kept my conversation focused on the idea that the concerns of our group were "world-like" in scope, and that just as they hoped a project of this kind would help with Hungary's social policy considerations, I had similar hope that it would be of value in America. A trustworthy rapport developed among us, although it took a bit to convince one of the group's members that I was not a spy of some sort, trying to involve myself with their work for surreptitious reasons.

The idea of organizing the concerns and efforts under the SRG banner was well accepted. We developed a research format and decided that a longitudinal study, one that stretched over a 10-year period, would be most effective. With this longer research period, we could most certainly make more legitimate assumptions about what we saw develop in Hungary, i.e., assumptions about how well capitalism mixed with socialism, what types of social policies were recommended, whether or not they were accepted by the government, how those accepted affected social problems and direct community service, and so on.

With these ideas in place, our major concern became obtaining funding. To these ends, I had some thoughts. The SRG had enormous potential. I believed that we could, with a minimal budget—our projected first year costs were $100,000—establish a successful research model in Budapest involving community members, politicians, academics and students. Therefore, similar, cost-effective projects could be organized in other countries. I also envisioned students across countries working at and comparing ideas as to the future potential of certain political, economic and social policy. With these points in mind, I thought we could bring our group's formation to the attention of those whose "bigger picture interests" might be connected to ours. Accordingly, I set out to seek funding.

Deciding who to approach with the SRG project took some thought. Much like my experiences with projects in the U.S., I realized that only people sensitive to the issues in the same way we were would support us. This would necessitate finding people interested in moving the world in a direction more focused on human concerns than on economic ones. This eliminated most traditional, corporate-like funding possibilities. It would also be helpful if, in addition to the human interest, funding sources had the money and power to move what we developed in Budapest out into the world. In short, we needed to locate people with significant amounts of money who had concerns about how they made that money.

As I contemplated these points, I thought perhaps there were individuals in the music world, big-time entertainers or rock groups whose songs often spoke to the injustices of the world, who might be interested in our project. There were, after all, several who had become spokespersons for human-focused movements. They might be willing to support a project as encompassing as ours. I contacted the European-based MTV organization, expressing the hope that they could act as a conduit to entertainers who could help us. I suggested that MTV could also become a part of the project, by reporting to their young audience what was happening with the project. I even suggested that, with their sponsorship, we could organize a first ever "rock conference" in Budapest, where entertainers could attend meetings to discuss how their interests might be channeled into projects like the SRG.

The people at MTV's headquarters in London initially liked the ideas. However, it became clear that they had difficulty providing access to entertainers about our ideas. They simply didn't see themselves in this role. This point, as well as the developing difficulties with new competitive- television programming, made them back away from assisting with the SRG efforts. They did tell me that if I was successful in organizing the entertainers on my own, they would be happy to provide support in advertising any conference activities, even to the extent of providing T-shirts, balloons, and so forth.

I continued to try to find ways to reach particular entertainers, but with little luck. I also began to reach out to several very wealthy industrialists who had expressed interests similar to those of the SRG project. I exchanged letters with three, world-renowned individuals, and although their correspondences were always encouraging, little was actually developed in terms of funding. I always had the feeling that, among other things, they were suspicious of an American, teaching with the University of Maryland, in the middle of this Hungarian/European project, i.e., was this a CIA ploy?

I continued to travel to Budapest with hopes of getting our project off the ground. I attempted to involve the University of Maryland with the project as well as the Rockefeller College of Public Affairs and Public Policy, from where I received one of my graduate degrees. In both cases, they seemed to be overwhelmed by the scope of the project, and any interest in the ideas got lost in decisions focused on what departments or what faculty might actually assume what responsibility.

I was disappointed with the results of my efforts, but there were some positive results. I was exposed to a great many experiences and made several lasting friendships along the way. Like with many of the other projects mentioned in this book, people continue to work at the ideas that were developed. And, I stay in contact with both the people and the ideas as we speak. In fact, it was because of my experiences in Budapest, as well as my other travels in Eastern Europe, that I was asked at times to talk about what I had learned. These opportunities, including being panelist in state department discussions about developments in Eastern Europe at our American consulate in Frankfurt, Germany, also provided some consolation for otherwise unsuccessful fundraising efforts.

Amidst my teaching and traveling, I was also exposed to the startling realities of war. I was in Germany during the Gulf War, and close to the military preparations for it. There was a very somber atmosphere on the bases, with security around the facilities at war-like levels, soldiers coming and going and their families and almost everyone else worrying about what was going to happen next. At times, I found the whole process unbelievable. It seemed like a game.

Initially, I found it hard to take the military exercises seriously, especially as I considered the Iraqi opposition. It was almost as if a professional football team was going through strenuous workouts to play against a team of high schoolers. But, for those whose lives centered on the activities, it was extremely serious. As I watched more of the jets, cargo planes and soldiers being readied, I eventually realized the seriousness as well. There was indeed a war on.

Toward the end of one term, I had an Army sergeant major in my class who was about ready to graduate when he was called to the desert front in the Gulf. In lieu of his last assignment, I asked him to prepare a piece on what he experienced when he first arrived there. He sent me a cassette and several pages describing what he saw developing. It was clear from his description of the sand, the heat and the failing military equipment, as well as the anxiety of his men, that what was happening was no game.

I had similar reactions when I was in Aviano, Italy, as the Bosnian crisis began to escalate. It was at that Air Force base where NATO headquarters would be situated and the daily reconnaissance flights and troop and cargo deployments kept the presence of war clear. The atrocities connected to the situation were reported daily, and they were enough to make even the most hawkish sick. I had occasion to travel to Bled, in Slovenia, where the war had actually begun before it moved quickly south into Yugoslavia. Bled is a small resort city, built by Marshall Tito in his ruling days. I got an eerie feeling sitting on the veranda at the golf course, sipping cocktails with Italians, Austrians and Yugoslavians, all of us dressed in our golf finery, knowing that a war was being fought only hours away. I also traveled further south to Zagreb, one of the former Yugoslavia's grand old cities. It wasn't devastated like the once beautiful Sarajevo and Dubrovnik, but the armed soldiers in the streets again reminded everyone there that a war continued, in this case, just minutes down the road.

The significance of these confrontations brought to light many considerations. The history of territorial disputes and religious hate among the factions involved in the Bosnian crisis seemed to imply that the crisis could never be settled. That same hate appeared to fester between the U.S. and Iraq, and it made me think that all negotiations in the Middle East and in the former Yugoslavia were more directed at managing war than in establishing peace.

I had other concerns as well. To what extent could Americans continue to protect interests abroad? And what were those interests anyway? Were we making the world safe for democracy, or were we maintaining capitalist interests and protecting vital resources for the sake of those interests? Were we hoping to free other countries with our efforts or were we the imperialists that many made us out to be? Were NATO and the United Nations actually post–World War II tools of American foreign economic policy, as many in Europe believed? These were only some of the questions raised by the conflicts, but they were important ones.

For me the questions again pointed to the necessity for us to have a better understanding of America. As complex as this would be, I couldn't help but think it was imperative for us to educate our public, particularly the young, to the dilemmas of capitalism which were so much a part of our lives. By doing this, we could address so many issues, war included. In fact, an undertaking of this sort should become a national mandate, so the occurrence of things as significant as war could be more clearly contemplated.

On the point of military directives, there didn't appear to be a soldier, general or private, worth his or her salt who didn't realize that their efforts were centered on American economic interests, and not on those of democracy. There was no delight taken in this realization. For soldiers, however, it's simply not within their job description to debate political or economic policy.

As had been my habit, I brought many of my experiences, including my concerns and thoughts, back to the classroom. My students enjoyed the discussions ranging from the issues of freedom and equality to the ideas being implemented in Budapest to the concerns of military intervention.

But, I was beginning to consider that I needed to re-think much of what I had experienced in light of what I had recently been exposed to. Although my students had no sense of it, I doubted whether I was as clear on issues as I could be. It had been four years since I left the United States, and a great deal had happened in that time. Experiences with the European Marxist-oriented systems added to my perspective on socialism and capitalism. I also had the connection with the military, and my thoughts on its significance as well as on war had been affected. Other ideas, like those related to biological explanations for behavior, and a more focused look at freedom and equality, had also grown in importance.

I was being encouraged by friends, colleagues and students as well that I should write a book about my experiences. I was beginning to believe that this was something I should seriously devote time to, something that could help me bring my thoughts and experiences together in a meaningful way.

At the same time, other things were happening. I was now attempting to raise funds for the Budapest project in the U.S. I knew that I needed to visit people to discuss this, so some travel was in the offing. Moreover, my teaching contract with the university needed to be altered. Technically, one can only teach with the university's European program for four years and then a break of a least one year must occur. Although it didn't seem possible, I had reached that four-year mark.

After some deliberation, I decided that, rather than involve myself with contract re-negotiations, I would take the year off to begin my book and tend to SRG funding matters. I also decided that I would return to Nevada, California and New York to do a bit of research with students at the universities I had attended. I knew that whatever I wrote would be directed at the lack of Marxist considerations in academic and public policy thought, so I reasoned that structuring questions directed at these considerations would be of significance. This would certainly help me determine the validity of many of my doubts.

I contacted my colleagues in the university systems and arranged to poll their students. It wouldn't be official research. Via a short questionnaire, I would simply ask students in the criminal justice and sociology disciplines about political, economic and social concepts. The responses would demonstrate how much or how little the students knew about liberal and conservative politics in America as well as democracy, capitalism, socialism and Marxism. My colleagues also became interested in the results.

The year off was a great deal of fun. I traveled stateside and polled not only students at universities in California, Nevada, New York and Connecticut, but other people along the way. To the point, I talked with everyone whose ear I could bend. Much as I suspected, most respondents showed that they knew little about the concepts that were helping to shape their worlds.

For the faculty membersI talked with, this fact was already very clear to them, and it was indeed worrisome. These faculty members also spoke about how poorly trained many teachers were in this area, which only added to their worries. Even though unofficial, my poll results supported the idea that a major re-examination of our educational processes was in order, both in a procedural and substantive sense.

I was unable to raise the funds for the SRG project stateside, but I did return to Hungary that year to spend time with my associates there. Although they were as disappointed as I with this news, they nonetheless intended to carry on with their research interests. I decided I would continue to try to raise funds, and, that more than likely, our relationship would be as concerned friends, rather than research colleagues.

I also traveled to Vancouver and Gran Canaria that year, and back to Austria and Italy. Throughout my travels, I attempted in the best Hemingway manner to write as much as I could, while I continued to talk with as many people as I could about the ideas that were important to me. Although those I spoke with supported my writing efforts, I couldn't organize my ideas into any worthwhile form. After eight months of trying, I had little to show in terms of writing my book.

While in Austria, and still attempting to write, I received a call from the director of the University of Maryland's European program. He asked me if I would like to travel to the university's Asian division, headquartered in Japan, to help develop and teach in a criminal justice program. He said the director of that division would be visiting in Europe and that I could talk with her directly about the possibilities. This proposition caught my interest.

By the time the director of the Asian division arrived in Germany I had convinced myself that this would be an experience I simply could not pass up. As with Europe before, I had never been to the Orient and this appeared the perfect opportunity. Given what I had learned while in Europe, I could only think that the Asian experience would offer more of the same. I decided to put my frustrations over the book on the back burner. I reasoned that perhaps I needed another "piece of the puzzle" to make it work.

After a brief return to New York, I boarded a flight to Osaka, Japan. I was to begin another round of teaching and traveling, and I was excited. I knew that, once again, my ideas and thoughts would be tossed about, but that this time, it would happen in a totally different culture.

Chapter 10

ASIA

After over a full day of flying, I landed in Osaka in the mid-afternoon. I was a bit weary from the flight, but as I departed the plane my spirits picked up as I again took stock of where I was. The symbols instead of letters on the advertisements, the sharp intonations of the language, the mass of Asian faces, everything was different. And, so was I.

My final destination in Japan was Okinawa, the small island south of the mainland. My flight there wasn't until the following afternoon so I had a bit of time to wander around after I checked into my hotel. As I went out into the streets to get a feel for the culture I could again sense being different. The feeling of being somewhere foreign was clearly evident.

I stopped in a large train station where people were coming and going at a pace similar to New York or Chicago. As I passed by a small deli-type shop, I looked at the assortment of fast food available. There were things I had never seen before. Out of my uncertainty, I chose a beef sandwich and coke. I left the station and strolled down the street, eating my late-afternoon snack as I went. I noticed that people kept glancing at me with what appeared to be a not-too-kind look, but I suspected that I either misinterpreted their look or they were simply suspicious of a larger, bearded American, wearing a long leather coat. Although both may have been true, I found out while speaking to an Englishman at the hotel that eating in the street was not something the Japanese favored. I recognized that I had a lot to learn.

The next day I arrived in Okinawa, the small island south of the mainland. I was greeted by a woman from the university, and as we drove to our office on the Kadena Air Force Base, she pointed out the military installations as we passed. It was very clear from their number that we had a huge military presence on the island.

The ride from the airport and through the city of Naha was relaxing. It was not hard to sense the "island feeling," and with the Pacific on one side and the China Sea on the other, I knew I was going to enjoy my stay. I was very happy as we passed by the beaches on the drive up-island, and even more so when we pulled into the main gate at the Kadena base, located just a pitching wedge away from the base's beautifully-landscaped golf course. When I was in Europe, I had informed the university that if I went to Asia, I wanted to go to the Okinawa site. I could enjoy the beaches, play golf and travel to any destination in the East. In other words, I thought it the ideal spot for a new work assignment. Fortunately, as it turned out, it was where they needed my help.

So much happened in the next two years that it's difficult to condense. On the academic level, I was teaching many of the same criminal justice courses I had taught in Europe, but I was also provided the opportunity to teach several sociology courses. This gave me the chance to stretch my thoughts into more broad-based issues, and I thoroughly enjoyed the challenge. One upper-level course in particular, called "The American Society," was perfectly suited to raise many of the points I had been struggling with in regards to the book. It was, in fact, partly due to the success of this course that my desire to writing was reinvigorated.

I enjoyed the teaching, as I always had. There was a good mix of American and Japanese students and the differences provided for interesting classroom conversations. Unlike in Europe, where many American students shared a European heritage, Japan presented a very different set of cultural traditions. This made the classroom a place for exploring some of those traditions, especially since many Americans and Japanese had little opportunity to talk with each other about issues like family disunity, poverty, crime, drug abuse, racism, etc.

This occurred despite the many years we Americans, in rather large numbers, had occupied the island. And, it was primarily a result of two things. First, the Japanese language is so difficult that most Americans only learn basic words. Conversely, most Japanese aren't fluent in English. This makes conversation on something as deep as social issues difficult. Second, the Japanese do not make it a habit, particularly with family issues, to talk about their social problems. In fact, many of the Japanese students were surprised about how open the American students were with discussions on social concerns. So, as any academic would hope, the classroom provided a good place for us all to get know each other better.

Okinawa itself was an interesting place. World War II memorials dotted the island, and it was unnerving to visit the battlegrounds or the suicide cliffs where thousands of lives had been lost. Whenever I visited these sites, now mostly covered by the beauty of the island, I often thought about how fortunate we Americans were in not having many of these places to call our own.

The people that I met, at least those I could communicate with, were very warm and hospitable. There was no hurry-up step to their work that was very much to my liking. From my first walks in the streets of Okinawa City, however, I remember thinking that with the different aromas and sounds and the different-looking people that it would be difficult for me to really understand the Japanese people. Even if I could reach a modicum of understanding, it would be difficult to compare their culture with ours. Their history was intricately tied to the principles of spirit and harmony. And, these principles played out in almost all of their everyday functions. This would be difficult to measure.

In other words, I began to consider whether my experiences in Japan would or could lend themselves to the concerns I had about America. What, I wondered, would my time in this part of the world tell me in terms of these concerns? I certainly had no answer, but the question seem to push me to other considerations. I was beginning to think that perhaps the two cultures were so different, especially given their basic principles, that attempts at borrowing or sharing ideas, particularly those related to social issues, might not be possible. But, I knew I had more to experience before I could be sure about my thoughts.

After the first-term break, I began to travel in Southeast Asia. I had a longstanding interest in visiting the small island of Palau in the South Pacific, dating back to reading about its "Walden Pond-like" struggle in the early 1980s. Therefore, I made it my initial trip outside of Japan.

Palau was a U.S. trust territory, which in the tangled language of post-war settlements, meant that it had U.S. protection but also a form of autonomy. The trust territory status was about to come to term, and the Palauans were deciding whether to continue with it or to cut themselves loose from all U.S. ties. In addition to this, the islanders had to decide whether, with either option they chose, to let the island remain as it was, i.e., protect its natural beauty, or develop it for commercial purposes. The focus of this "commercial interest versus natural beauty" dilemma was Palua's naturally deep harbor. Palua was located in an ideal spot both for tourism and strategic military operations and the existence of "the perfect" harbor added to the islanders' deliberations.

As economic and political interests in the Pacific had been rapidly developing so did the interests in Palau. The U.S. wanted them to opt to renew their trust status giving us access to their locale and port, or to at least provide us with some preferential harbor rights if there was a trust separation. Some feared that in either case the focus would be on developing the island more than on maintaining its natural beauty. Others feared that without attention to development, the island would suffer financial ruin. I was very much interested in what direction the islanders might proceed.

While having dinner on my first night in Palau, I noticed an American man sitting alone, reading a paper as he ate. After paying my bill, I stopped by to introduce myself and to see if I could ask him a few questions. He was very gracious and we sat and talked for some time. He was a lawyer, one among the surprisingly large number of one hundred lawyers who had settled on the island. With only 18,000 inhabitants on this small, seemingly-remote island, this was indeed a high number. He told me that the inordinate number of "legal eagles" was due to the growing significance of the island's future. It seemed that not only was the island's future at stake, but that the issues being raised were having an impact on what might happen in other places in Southeast Asia as well. I immediately sensed that I needed to know more about what the lawyer was saying.

He gave me the name of another lawyer who could shed more light on these matters, suggesting I contact him the next day. I was able to meet with this man the following night and he provided me with some very provocative information. He told me the greatest threat to those who were fighting to maintain the natural beauty of the island and opposing heavy commercial development was not, as I had suspected, from the Americans. Rather, the most significant threat was coming from the Taiwanese.

It seemed that many rich Taiwanese, with the fear of an impending Chinese takeover in Taiwan, were trying to invest their money elsewhere. One of the places they were doing this was in Palau. They would come to the island, make friends with the natives by giving them money and cars and then either try to buy their land outright, or at least convince them to go into business together.

The rule in many nations is that businesses have to be developed in conjunction with a national partner, allowing nationals to prosper while keeping competing international interests somewhat in check. The Taiwanese were suspected of trying to gain bargaining power over U.S. or Chinese activities in terms of their respective interests in Palau's strategic location. If they could obtain a foothold on the island, then irrespective of what materialized, they would most likely benefit from that position, if only from the increase in property value. The situation reminded me a bit of our relationship with the American Indian.

I listened to this, not sure that all of it was true, but clearly understanding the logic of what was being said. What I was hearing severely jogged my senses about the situation on the island. There were major players involved, with major, but not necessarily similar interests. China could be connected, if only through the fact that it was seen, particularly by the Taiwanese, as the emerging power. And Japan, who shared a very inhospitable relationship with China, was also connected simply due to its interests in shifting world power.

And, of course, there was the U.S., whose economic and concomitant military interests were clearly of concern. This mix of interests then, although clouded to the naked eye, was playing itself out on the small island of Palau.

It wasn't as if I hadn't read or heard about these interests in Southeast Asia. But, coming face to face with their realities made their presence more provocative. I immediately saw the global power struggle more clearly, and I also recognized its importance. China represented one fifth of the world's population. An alliance, trade or otherwise, with Russia, India and even Africa was something that could happen. This would create a coalition of producers and consumers equaling two thirds of the world's population.

The Japanese, although economic competitors with the U.S., still needed to keep us close as their long-standing foe China began to flex its muscles. In light of this, as well as the U.S.'s own economic interests, a U.S.-Japan coalition almost had to happen. Nonetheless, given the numbers of people and resources, it seemed that power would shift toward the China-led affiliations, with the U.S. and Japanese no longer in a position of dominance. And, thinking in these terms, the newly formed European Union would be in last position in the standings of international competition.

This was all speculation for sure. But, as I pondered the possibilities, I thought how tremendously interesting my trip to Palau had become. I spent the next four days exploring the island, snorkeling in the beautiful ocean waters and talking with the island people. Most gave me their version of what the lawyers had already told me, and they were clearly uneasy about what would happen with their island. But, whatever happened, the overall sentiment was that life would go on.

An interesting side note occurred when I visited Palau's legislative and judicial hall. Because of the lack of written contracts for native land exchanges and the increasing worth of the property, especially in relationship to what the Taiwanese were doing, land disputes filled the court dockets. An American lawyer I spoke with outside the hall remarked that he was afraid all he did in Palau was teach people how to "bend the truth" in terms of what they remembered about what was theirs and how they had obtained it.

Without any written agreements this was the only way to come to some understanding about what had happened in land exchanges. He shook his head as he mused over the lawyers' legacy. The islanders had gotten good lessons in how to lie more than anything else.

What I learned on my trip to Palau helped me frame much of what I saw in my future travels. Southeast Asia was developing at a rapid pace, and the changes were everywhere. In the context of my concerns over what was happening in the U.S., I couldn't forget what I was seeing here. America was America, and we had our issues, but the rest of the world was turning as well.

I made trips to extravagant Hong Kong and the gambling port of Macua. I went to Korea and Taiwan and I saw that the people I had once thought of as all the same were indeed quite different. The language, customs and even the smells coming from the storefronts were different. I spent time in Bangkok and rural Thailand and the distinction between the overcrowded, heavily shopped, smog-filled streets of the high rise city and the outlying thick, green countryside was fascinating. I traveled through the waterways where the less than privileged of Bangkok lived on, and practically in, the water in small, wooden stilted huts with no sanitation or running water. It was common, everyday living for them—children were being borne, wives talked with wives, neighbors liked or disliked neighbors, and so on. But, it was so different from what I knew. As I passed by the people, living as they did, I could only wonder what our (my) political, economic and social concerns had to do with these people. What I was seeing made me feel ignorant about so many things.

My trip to Burma was probably the most memorable. What I saw there made me think even harder about what I didn't and couldn't know about the people in this part of the world. Traveling from the low-rise capital city of Yangon, I went to various Buddhist temples with the guide I hired explaining the significance of Buddha as we went. The temples ranged from park-like sites with huge statues of Buddha figures to small, remote places in the woods with only parts of the Buddha (a tooth, a hand, sometimes only a replica of such a part) on display. Wherever they were located, people stopped to pray, and I was amazed at how much they were willing to give of their small incomes at these temples. An income for a year can be less than

$500, but donations were made nonetheless. Although I sensed that the military regime was also benefiting from the people's devout beliefs, my subtle queries regarding that notion were hardly acknowledged by my guide.

During my stay we visited cigar-making and wood-carving factories located in the outskirts of the city. In these places young people, many of them teenaged women, worked continuously at their tasks, turning out products that could be bought for one twentieth of what you might pay in a western market. We also visited an eyelash factory, owned by my guide, where animal hair was turned into eye lashes for dolls being manufactured in Thailand. This was imagery that certainly spoke to the western workers' worries about cheap labor.

We shopped at a large outdoor market in the city, where the people, especially young children, came up to us and stared as if they hadn't seen a western face before. Come to find out, some of them hadn't, especially one bearded like mine. The people seemed enamored with our presence, and they struggled to get into the pictures we were taking. It evoked mixed sensations in me; I was a celebrity without any real claim to fame.

My guide brought me to the home of a native family. The home was basically one large room partitioned with bamboo sheets. We were welcomed with root tea and large, hand-rolled cigars, and we sat and drank tea and smoked with the man of the house while his wife and children sat by our sides. They were very gracious hosts and attempted to answer my questions about everyday life in a way that insulted neither their homeland nor my curiosity. I wasn't sure that everything was being interpreted exactly as it was intended, but I felt a sense of honesty about the people, and that was satisfying enough for me. I also remember feeling that what they had or didn't have was clearly visible, which made pretense of little concern.

We also visited a Buddhist monastery, serene to the extent of being a bit eerie, where monks and those training to become monks strolled along with very little conversation taking place. We joined individuals in a meditation room where they sat or walked in a very slow circular manner for hours without speaking. We ate lunch at the monastery, a very basic rice dish, and I asked a monk who decided to join us several politically-pointed questions. As with the spiritual experiences in new age California, I was wondering to what political/ economic/societal ends the people at the monastery might aspire to. I can't quote the monk's response exactly, but in kind words he told me that we were at a place where such ideas were not of primary importance.

Perhaps the most startling sight of my visit was a large fishing industry at the edge of the city. Here sandpans moved slowly through the muddy waters, with men catching fish, dumping their catches into large, rattan baskets, then paddling their boats totteringly to shore. The baskets were then, in a chain-like fashion, passed from one man to the next, up a steep, muddy bank, to the factory where the fish were cleaned and cut.

The factory was a huge building, with fish parts strewn everywhere and where marketeers and the fish sellers meandered about. The street side of the factory was surrounded by small stands, where people sold everything from beads to iced water—water dripping over a block of ice. The smells and the noises were incredible. And, in the background of all this was a constant, song-like drone, coming from loudspeakers attached to poles, with words, I was told, that encouraged everyone that their work was good, for them and for Buddha. The people, especially by our standards, were poor and dirty, and I felt both sad and uncomfortable as I tried not to act like a voyeur as I passed their stands.

These experiences punctuated my feelings of being a foreigner in this part of the world. I had little, if any, connection to these people. Their lives, their thoughts, their...well almost everything, was not at all related to what we do or how we live in America.

The morning before we departed from Burma, we stopped at a newly built country club on the way to the airport. It was certainly a contrast to the fish factory tour. The guide had never been to the club before and he was unsure of how to act once we arrived. The place was clearly for the elite, marking the more than evident distinction between the haves and the have-nots. This prompted me again to consider my being different. Although I saw this distinction, and had some understanding as to its sources, the challenge of responding to it in a place like Burma was well beyond my reach.

Throughout my travels, things happened that kept the presence of China close at hand. For example, upon returning to Japan from a Burma-to-Bangkok trip, my flight was delayed because of the escalating Chinese military exercises over Taiwan's claim to autonomy. And everywhere, people talked of how rapidly China was developing and what an awesome power it represented. This worried some, in particular the Japanese, whose long-standing animosities with the Chinese gave them cause for anxiety. The "sleeping giant" was clearly awakening and what I sensed from this was an unsettled atmosphere of both fear and recognition.

I had the opportunity to visit the small city of Zhuhai, in southern China. It was on this brief excursion that I heard some interesting comments about China's status. On the invitation of a businessman/friend from Hong Kong, who also owned a factory on mainland China, I went to visit his business and to play golf at a beautiful, almost totally hand-carved course, located on the outskirts of the city. This experience was an event of its own, but at the days end, I was able to chat with our two golfing companions, both Chinese businessmen, about my thoughts on China. We discussed many things, but I found their comments on how differently they viewed issues like human rights as compared to Americans most interesting.

They clearly didn't like Americans commenting on human rights issues when it appeared to them that Americans could not address their own shortcomings in this area. For them, their cultural traditions led them to different conclusions of what was morally and civicly just. Both men believed that, even in the sense of Tiananmen Square, young people had to develop an understanding that not everything the western world had to offer could or should be immediately available to them. This meant that the elders had to discipline the younger generation, much like a parent would any child.

In relationship to the young people's behavior this could mean that, as with the square incident, the discipline would be quite harsh. What was important to understand was that the state's reaction was not only a measure pointed at the young people's behavior, but also at the long-term goals of the society. The Chinese were attempting to mix dangerous capitalist elements into their society, and this had to be done slowly and carefully. And, discipline was, at times, simply necessary.

I knew that if I had been one of the young people in the square I would have found this explanation inciting. But, as I sat with these men, I could understand their logic. It made even more sense as they talked about how important harmony was to their culture. Relating this to my new age experiences, I had some notion of what this implied, but I clearly couldn't relate to it as they did. These men saw China as trying to integrate this harmony within the hectic context of economic and political development. This complicated matters even more for them, often making their efforts appear inconsistent or convoluted, especially to non-understanding westerners. It was explained to me, however, that the Chinese were not overly concerned about the appearance of "making mistakes." In fact, they weren't at all fond of that word description. Instead, they chose to look at what they did in terms of advancing their civilization's power. Whatever happened in that context would not be looked upon as a mistake, but as a necessary part of that advancement. I remember thinking how interesting it would be for us in America to consider our future policies in a similar light.

I couldn't make a solid judgment on their comments, but I was impressed with what I heard. Amidst the scattered newsprint, reporting and propaganda on China, I knew that this civilization understood many things, perhaps to a greater extent than we did. What I was being told made me feel that, despite the overwhelming difficulties facing them, they were definitely on route toward increasing power. I wasn't exactly sure where this put us as Americans. But, as the words of my dinner companions implied, the Chinese really didn't care.

I also asked these men about the coalitions I had considered while visiting Palau. If China aligned itself with India and Africa and even Russia, what could that spell in terms of world power? They agreed that, especially in terms of trade, this was a most logical link for China to pursue, and something it could do. The result of this link, even though it would be a complex and slowly developing process, was something that Japan, the U.S. and Europe would have to contend with.

The recognition of this possibility made me again consider where this put us, and how important and sensitive our relationship with China had become. I thought of China, with its size, population and power, as a conduit to the others in India, Africa and Russia. I realized that this was as much speculation as anything, yet I even imagined China in the role of the U.S., with business interests and military bases across the world. It was a very thought-provoking dinner conversation, indeed.

As I traveled and taught and digested what I was seeing and hearing, I could see that we westerners had a lot to learn about what was happening in the East. The ideals of socialism and communism, whether seen through the eyes of Mao, the gun barrels of a military or the prayers to Buddha, were important in terms of the political, economic and social relationships at work in many of the countries in Asia. And, this reinforced the idea that we needed to understand these concepts.

In terms of the places and things I saw, I couldn't really measure the successes and I wasn't sure whether things could be better, or how much worse they could get. But, the people seemed motivated by what was happening in their world, although I suspected many knew very little about where they were headed. I supposed that, in this sense, they were in a position similar to Americans.

My travels now affected me differently than before. Rather than thinking about looking elsewhere, I now had the sensation of being pushed back to my own culture by my experiences. I had stumbled across the realization that, despite my frustrations with what we did, I belonged in America. I was saturated with thoughts, and it was only there, if anywhere, that these thoughts would have any practical application. This realization hit me with such force that it dampened my spirit for more travel. I had, I believed, seen enough.

Many years had passed since I left my hometown, and a multitude of experiences had unfolded, both in a professional and personal sense. I had lost my father and my mother had been living alone for the past year. In this regard, I was feeling a very strong pull to return to New York. Almost as strong a pull was coming from my desire to finally write the book I had been considering for so long. I had lived through more than my share of experiences and conversed with many different people about many different things. I finally felt settled enough to put forth the effort a book would demand. And, in recognizing my "Americanness," I began to consider the possibilities of re-involving myself with the issues that continued to concern me, issues that were part and parcel of being an American.

As I went about my daily routine back on Okinawa of teaching, reading, golfing, going to the beach, I could feel a great surge of emotion pulling me back to the U.S. Without being certain what it would bring, I simply knew it was time to return. After almost two years in Southeast Asia and five years in Europe, I decided I would move back stateside. In May 1997, over 20 years after I entered prison, I was going home—a well-degreed, well-experienced, well-traveled individual, someone who was again going to try to make a difference. Hopefully, I thought, writing this book would be a step in that direction.

PART FIVE

Chapter 11

CONCLUSION

I've waited quite some time to get to this conclusion. First, I needed to sort out my experiences, for the most part, to establish my credibility as an American social thinker. I hope by now I have proven my worth. I touched upon many issues in the book. They included the problems of inequality and its effects on opportunity, as well as the law and the criminal justice system. The problems with education, particularly its substantive neglect of important civic concerns, were also noted. I also raised issues that pertained to community organization and project development, and generally, how difficult social work is in America. And, I raised points about how our culture might be viewed by those in other countries. Suffice it to say that, from my time in prison to my traveling and learning about the world, the issues could fill a book.

In covering the issues, a theme was developed. The theme was that because so much of what happens in America can be linked to capitalism, a critical analysis of capitalism is critical to understanding America, most particularly if we wish to make America better. Importantly, this analysis also speaks to a construct under which a significant portion of the world operates. Therefore, as this analysis is fairly easy to grasp, we should simply know more about it. I hope, as with the social thinker appellation, that this theme was given support throughout the book.

But, now the focus becomes how to conclude the book, how to capsulize the experiences and how to deal with the issues raised through them in a meaningful way. What should I say? In what direction should I proceed? Certainly, the reader is anticipating something more about how we might make what I've suggested happen.

Relative to this I entertained several options. One possibility was to choose a highly theoretical conclusion. This would mean that my experiences and the ideas that I have been exposed to would be interwoven with hypotheses that parallel those experiences and ideas. For example, I could tie my criminal behavior to theories like Edwin Sutherland's theory on "differential association." In this theory, individuals generally learn from their environment and relationships in that environment to become criminal, in the same way any other behavior is learned. I could also relate the problems I have seen within the American system to Max Weber's thoughts on the nature of bureaucracies and how they unavoidably develop within society. Or, I could discuss Marxism more fully, reviewing concepts like alienation and surplus labor in the context of my experiences. Using these theoretical ideas, I could talk about and debate their tenets, as well where their respective applications might lead us.

I could also have opted to write a conclusion that intricately details what we should do about the problems I have pointed to in the book. For example, I could talk more about the concept of drug legalization, outlining clearly its benefits over our current policy. I could also talk about developing a new tax system, which could be focused on redistributing corporate wealth to help cure social ills. I could talk about altering the legal system, from an adversarial one where money means almost everything, to a more fact-finding, court work-group approach. This is, by the way, what most poorer people get anyway. I could also talk about rearranging the health care system and the criminal justice system in ways that would direct our attention to how people should be treated in the most free and most powerful country in the world. I could talk about addressing our dual labor force--primary for those best connected to our opportunity structure, secondary for others--which would mean relating it to our dual educational system and the issues of class distinctions and inequality.

Detailing these problems and the related policy concerns, especially given what must take place at both economic and political levels, would indeed make interesting reading.

However, neither of these choices seemed consistent with the tenor of the book. Simply put, the book was a story about experiences, and these dissertation-like conclusions seemed out of character with its style. Accordingly, although I possess a fair amount of knowledge in terms of theories and potential courses of action, I would rather defer to the experts who have written extensively on these subjects. The works of individuals like Richard Quinney, David Gordon, Noam Chomsky and Marx himself, to mention only a few, would be more appropriate in bringing the details of such considerations clearly to light. So, I will only suggest that you read them.

What makes more sense for my conclusion, and what is actually more on point with what I really wanted to talk about, involves a conversation about logic. For as I continue to talk with people—family, friends and individuals I happen to meet—and as I begin again to teach classes at a state university and involve myself with academic and community projects, I cannot escape the dulling feeling that we have truly lost contact with our collective logic.

What I mean is that we seem to be at an illogical point in America where the political arena clearly doesn't represent the people's interests (money is such a factor in moving politicians and legislation that you're simply a fool to think otherwise); where less than 50 percent of the people vote for our leaders and even fewer trust our government; where the media, still laying claim to be being the public's conscience, no longer concerns itself with integrity but seems to take some comfort in reporting on how it's being lost; where the family is expected to instill values that don't exist in the real world and parents are expected to work their lives away trying to make ends meet; where crime and violence are rampant and some suggest that America is having a war in the streets; where a concern like the overall health care of the nation is poorly tended to; where education seems to have little value other than to point people at jobs which are sold to foreign countries just like any other product; where...

Pick up a book, a magazine or a newspaper. Talk to your neighbor. Better yet, look in your own mirror or out your own back door. The problems are as real as problems get. Yet, while they occur, most of us seem to be backing up, pulling away and moving inward, whether out of disdain over the affairs of state or complacency, or a combination of both. It doesn't take a genius to recognize that as this happens, we are in serious jeopardy of losing what we have come to see as our own. We are behaving illogically, in the face of what, in the most free and most powerful country in the world, is a precarious situation.

We are, in fact, amidst a national identity crisis and in need of some form of political, economic and social psychoanalysis. Unfortunately, there is no one shrink who can untangle our thoughts. In a Hitchcock-like state of paradoxes, we seem afraid to recognize the identity we see before us, denying that we are part of it, denying our ability to make any difference, denying any need to confront what we see.

Frankly, the illogic of the situation scares me. Strangely enough, more so than when I went to prison. I'm scared for the American people, about the future of our society and about the ability of our leadership to take us there with dignity and design. I'm scared as I see the distorted picture of what America ought to be and what we actually are. My experiences and my travels have made me realize how great it is to be an American, but my doubts and fears about America have grown accordingly. I wish I didn't have nagging thoughts and feelings, but I do.

In coming to grips with this situation and in trying to better understand our illogical circumstance, it is fair to ponder how this all happened. How did we get this way? In keeping with Marx's thoughts, it might well be that a capitalist system grows so exploitive of the general public that those with the power will do anything, including deceiving others and manipulating the truth, to avoid "letting on" what is happening. This, for the most part, leaves people "in the dark" and helps explain the vagaries of political conversation, the interconnectedness of politics to economics and the disconnectedness of both in terms of resolving social problems. It, in essence, makes the illogical quite logical in that being in the dark is a logical consequence of our capitalist system. However, I am unconvinced of this, particularly as a sole explanation for our circumstance.

Given the substantial accomplishments in our country and the world, and taking into consideration our fortunate history, it is fair to believe that we came to ignore the importance of profit motive in our analysis of America. Despite the worries of some of our forefathers, the warnings of people like Tocqueville and Marx and our ongoing struggles with freedom and equality, it is very possible that we saw ourselves so differently, so independent and so joined in the experiment of democracy, that we refused to entertain anything else. In this light our spirit, energy and most importantly our successes were so ignited and fueled by the democratic ideology that there was little room for alternative thought. We perceived ourselves on such a strong course that the course itself and the perception of where it should lead became our master.

My experiences have contributed to supporting this notion. In the mix of my criticisms and the shortcomings of my efforts, I can still see America as a country whose history is as great as great can be, and as a country filled with the potential for a great future. I think of this possibility in terms of our country's character—young, borne of revolution, fortunate through our history and still wrestling with our potential.

If this is the case, if we are not locked into our current state of illogic by an all-consuming system, but more by oversight, then we have the potential to change and avoid, as some suggest, inevitable self-destruction. But, what will it take to realize our potential, to, for all intents and purposes, grow up?

It is not hard to imagine that what we choose to do, save only hoping that time will make the difference, will take tremendous effort and energy. We are faced with a problem that seems almost impossible to address. We live in a system that is capitalist, but most people don't really know what that means. Unfortunately, most of these same people, who should at least understand the implications of our capitalism, don't, because our educational process simply doesn't focus on it. Remember, most teachers aren't that familiar with a critical analysis of capitalism either. Furthermore, both our political and economic leaders generally have their interests intricately tied to the capitalist system. Even if they understood the analysis, and, as with educators, this is a legitimate concern, they would be hard pressed to challenge their own vested interests.

So where does this leave us? Am I now saying what I denied before? Am I saying that the system has such a powerful life of its own that it cannot be altered? That we are what we are and we should accept it and move on accordingly?

Well, maybe yes. Maybe we can't do much about the current state of social problems in America. In fact, maybe things aren't so bad, and maybe, in time, things will get better. But, on that same note, we should at least be given the opportunity to better understand what we are willing to accept. We should be given all the variables that relate to understanding our system, which in turn would give us the chance to make decisions about our future for ourselves. So in a sense, we should be seeking an understanding of capitalism simply because we should have it, whether we change things or not.

But we are still left with how we push for this understanding. What will an effort of this sort look like? If the political and economic arenas are as tightly tied to the system as suggested, at whom do we propel such an effort?

Initially, it seems that we, the public, must take the responsibility. We must call for a new dialogue about America that will include consideration of the ideas and implications attached to a critical analysis of capitalism. These are ideas and implications that will help us demystify what we do in America. They will help us clarify what we did in our past, and what we might do in our future.

This will take, as this book hopefully suggested, a review of many concerns, from the tenets of what Jefferson saw as a great democracy to the principles of what Marx saw as a capitalist nation. It will involve the organization of theories and strategies, a large-scale endeavor, where all the pieces of what might be considered the American puzzle will be examined. This process is not a panacea for all our ills, but it is certainly one that will help us look for cures. So again, the challenge itself involves making the call and asking for clarification of what has been, is and will happen in America.

The exact construct of this effort is difficult to detail, and I am not proposing to have the blueprint. But, the design, in and of itself, should be considered as a good portion of the challenge. Perhaps the more difficult part of the challenge has already been mentioned— at whom do we propel it?

In thinking about this, difficulties become apparent. Again there are the vested interests at both the political and economic levels. However, there are at least some in both arenas who recognize how intimately linked their accomplishments are with what the American people have, for so long, believed about America. These individuals should have no trouble acknowledging the tremendous social energy it has taken to survive thus far, and they can help with the tremendous effort it will take to carry this energy on into the future. In terms of creating a new dialogue, we need to seek these individuals out.

But given what we see today, we know these people are few. There needs to be others. And, where will these others come from? One consideration seems to help with an answer. For if, as I have so claimed, the American public hasn't been adequately informed of what a critical analysis of capitalism entails, then the public itself will have to become more savvy about it. This being the case, logic should tell us that the educational arena, where ideas are developed and discussed, is where our focus should be. The educational arena is best suited to both accept the challenge and help define its character.

It would be through education that such a monumental task of re-energizing and restructuring America would best be centered. It is there where the search for and research of ideas can best be initiated and where a dialogue for our future generations can best be facilitated. These are, after all, the objectives of education.

This suggestion, of course, is not without its own set of difficulties. It means we must create a new dialogue with long range intent. What we do will take time and educators, teachers and administrators alike cannot give in to short term fixes. Moreover, it will take the willingness of these people to accept this responsibility and to accept that they themselves may not know, at this juncture, enough about a critical analysis of capitalism. Developing educational strategies that include this analysis will be, for many, a learning process. Certainly this will be difficult, perhaps involving workshops and seminars for educators. But, in the spirit of education, this is something that should be welcomed. Almost everyone in education understands that it is in the "looking where you don't know" that learning best occurs.

Though complex, especially in light of the continual corporatization of American education, this could be such an exciting venture, perhaps the most exciting in our lifetime. Just think educators, a chance to bring theory more close to practice, a chance to become a more effective teacher, a chance to gain more respect!

Secondary and post-secondary institutions, and the students enrolled in them, could join in the search for what a new America might look like. Along with the social scientists and social philosophers, they could bring the ideals of democracy and the pragmatics of capitalism into focus. And, along with the community, they might create different ideas on how to live and how to become more interpersonally and civically connected.

There already is evidence that learning is being affected in ways that are conducive to this challenge. As an example, I recently visited an elementary school where the daily focus is to prompt youngsters to think about what they do and to consider their actions and especially the words they use in terms of who they are and how they relate to other people. The youngsters seem to be getting a better sense of themselves and those around them.

In this case alone, couldn't we develop and then plug in concepts related to capitalism and democracy to get young people to begin to think about the world they must live in? Couldn't we instill in them a sense of how principles like freedom and equality work, including our own shortcomings, and how systems work for and against the realization of these principles? Couldn't we begin to develop a dialogue pointed in this direction so that when people completed secondary school and were responsible enough to vote they had a solid sense of what we can do in America?

Couldn't we continue this focus as people went on to post-secondary institutions? It would be easy to implement mandated courses, perhaps one in the first year and another toward graduation, where students concentrated on social, political and economic issues with the idea of fueling an ongoing and continually developing dialogue.

And, couldn't we even develop a similar process for the general community, holding classes and seminars for that purpose and allowing for time to be taken from work to do so? Couldn't we insist that educators, within the context of their research endeavors, develop projects that reflect upon social policy in ways that consider liberal, conservative and radical perspectives alike, providing us, the public, the chance to review the differences while broadening our understanding of the choices?

There are some who would believe that what I am proposing is impossible, that I am naive and that it is illogical to ask that, we tip our system on its head to see what happens. The uncertainty of what is being proposed is not what a society, especially one as successful as ours, will endorse. Again, I can only offer the logic of what has been presented, and suggest that, particularly given our current state of affairs, we are being tipped anyway. To think that we can straighten ourselves out without considering what has been proposed is in itself naive.

Moreover, I think it is important to consider that we have sent people to the moon and beyond, something only several generations ago was as far from possible as the stars themselves seemed to be. In our own generation, we have seen advancements in technology that have gone beyond our imaginations. It seems hard to believe then, that we cannot simply come to a better understanding of capitalist America, that we cannot create a dialogue about who we are and where we are going. Rather than being seen as an impossibility, it should be, in the most free and most powerful country in the world, a national mandate.

I note, however, that we do not have to take this new direction, that we don't have to face what I have referenced as a national identity crisis. We can stay on the course we are on, not troubling ourselves with admitting to anything, especially something that comes in the form of an arduous examination into our collective selves. At least for now, for the immediate years ahead, the world will most likely continue to turn as we know it. We can carry on the bravado of being number one, of being the best, denying what in fact we see—in essence, that such an identity crisis exists.

But again, look around you. This bravado belies a weakening spirit. And, you and I know that this circumstance does not bode well, that it likely represents an ominous portent of things to come.

In fact, it may be that it is already too late. The dye may be cast, the corner already turned, the system simply too great. But, I'm supposing this hasn't happened. And given this, I'm supposing that people are so confused, so scared and so angry from the predicaments they are in, from the nonsensical situations and illogical circumstances that they see, that they would be willing to listen to what has been, in the past, largely ignored. Ideas once considered inconsiderable, will now seem worth listening to. Indeed, now is the right time to clear the air.

What this conclusion points to then—what, in fact, might be considered the "raison d'être" for this book—is not a promise for any panacea, but a call for a collective effort, generated by public concern and centered on the logic of developing a new dialogue about America. It is by no means a new call, it comes from as far back as our revolutionary beginnings and extends throughout our history. But, as our vision has become clouded, I am making the call again, referenced in a different way, the way it came to me, with the hope of rejuvenating the spirit it will take to address the call.

But, in addition to this call, let this book also serve as a warning. The warning suggests that lest we take up the chore of untangling democratic ideals and capitalist tenets, the lines of confusion that permeate our system will continue to grow. More disconcerting, we may well continue to push each other into what Orwell referenced as a state of doublethink: "to know and not to know, to be conscious of complete truthfulness while telling carefully constructed lies, to hold simultaneously two opinions which cancel out, knowing both to be contradictory and believing in both of them, to use logic against logic, to repudiate morality while laying claim to it."

I think we can all agree that it would be a shame to let this happen.

Please think about this, as I hope you will think about the entire book. Read the words that follow, and then think even more. Recognize your own past in social-thinker terms. You also have experiences with America. Begin to seek out on your own ways to better understand your country. Remember, you have a part in shaping the future. There is much to do, much more to talk about. But, for now, this is all I have to say:

> *Enlighten the people generally, and tyranny and oppression of body and mind will vanish like evil spirits at the dawn of day. Although I do not, with some enthusiasts, believe that the human condition will ever advance to such a state of perfection as that there shall no longer be pain or vice in the world, yet I believe it susceptible of much improvement, and the diffusion of knowledge among the people is to be the instrument by which it is to be effected.*
>
> *Finally, whether peace is best preserved by giving energy to the government or information to the people. This last is the most legitimate engine of government. Educate and inform the whole mass of people. Enable them to see that it is their interest to preserve peace and order, and they will preserve them...They are the only sure reliance for the preservation of our liberty.*
>
> Thomas Jefferson

AFTERWARD

My editor suggested that I write an afterward, providing additional information about what I'm doing these days, perhaps tying up loose ends or providing insight into my personal self. For her, more needed to be said.

I debated this idea with her. My contention was that in the three years it took to complete the book, I had sufficiently sorted through my thoughts and ideas, and said what I needed to say. Moreover, I reasoned that her suggestion was already being tended to, as I was beginning another book, a collection of vignettes and short stories based on more personal recollections. As we talked about the matter, it appeared that we were both right. Readers might want to know more about what I'm doing these days and how my struggles are playing out as I've settled back into the American experiment. But, at least at this point, they surely didn't want to read another book. So, what follows is only a bit more on what is happening in my life.

As I mentioned in the text, I continue to teach part-time at a public university in New York. I enjoy my role as adjunct faculty because it allows me to choose courses and talk about issues and ideas accordingly.

I will also begin lecturing in Italy this coming year at the University of Italy in Udine. A new school for interpreters and translators designed in part to provide the students with a more substantive understanding of the English language has been established there. The director, a close friend of mine, has asked me to lecture based on my experiences, expertise and the ideas expressed in this book, in the Language, Institutions and Culture Program at the school. I'm excited about this opportunity.

I'm also involved with radio. Phil Pisani and I have developed a weekly program that addresses a variety of social and community issues, often featuring live interviews with members of the community. Although our program is only local, I enjoy the medium and will continue to invest my time in the talk-radio process.

A significant amount of my energy is being channeled into a new project that lends itself to some of the ideas I've expressed in this book. I have been given the opportunity to develop a community center in a small, industrialized section of upstate New York. With the support of the local corporations the center will provide the community—mostly the workers in the industries—with services like child care, counseling and dispute resolution. The idea of getting corporations to take more responsibility for the community and the focus on labor issues are certainly consistent with the tenor of the book.

Hopefully with the success of the book and related talks and lectures, I would also like to revive other projects. In particular I would like to see time devoted to developing concepts like the project in Hungary—a social problem research center staffed by students that can be linked across countries (perhaps getting people in the music business to help examine social problems via their involvement in a rock conference.) There is also a need to develop more programs that could help transition juveniles in trouble into educational opportunities (perhaps getting the adult inmate population via inmate welfare funds to sponsor such projects.)

In essence then, I'm still working at the same old things— teaching, facilitating community projects and developing ideas. I expect this will never change.

My mother is fine and our relationship buoys both our spirits. I still have the urge to "go" somewhere at times, but I sense that this is more the result of having done this for so long. And, perhaps, my "not going" is a function of my age as well.